18.95

Liszt

Unlocking the Masters Series, No. 18

Liszt

A Listener's Guide to His Piano Works

John Bell Young

AMADEUS PRESS
An Imprint of Hal Leonard Corporation
New York

Published in 2009 by Amadeus Press
An Imprint of Hal Leonard Corporation
7777 West Bluemound Road
Milwaukee, WI 53213

Trade Book Division Editorial Offices
19 West 21st Street, New York, NY 10010

Printed in the United States of America

Book design by Snow Creative Services

Library of Congress Cataloging-in-Publication Data

Young, John Bell.
Liszt : a listener's guide to his piano works / by John Bell Young.
p. cm. – (Unlocking the masters series ; no. 18)
Includes bibliographical references.
ISBN 978-1-57467-170-4 (alk. paper)
1. Liszt, Franz, 1811–1886. Piano music. 2. Piano music—19th century—History and criticism. I. Title.

ML410.L7Y68 2009
786.2092–dc22

2008045426

www.amadeuspress.com

For Joe and Veronique Fabio

Contents

Acknowledgments

Writing about music, or any work of art governed by abstraction, is no easy task. One is as easily persuaded by force of habit as by long-held beliefs in the veracity of a point of view, as if objectivity were the only thing that mattered.

But as any musicians worth their salt know only too well, there are no ivory towers: music is so complex and abundant as to invite any number of perspectives. And where those perspectives are as informed as they are imaginative, they are worthy of contemplation.

Much the same can be said of any artistic endeavor, and writing is no exception. I am indebted for their assistance and advice to a number of friends and colleagues, several of whom did not live to see the completion of this project nor were even aware that what I learned from them would contribute to it so substantially.

Above all there is my late mother, Dorothy Burgess Young, without whose support and unflinching belief in my abilities I could never have written this volume, or even so much as played a single note at the piano.

There are in addition a number of individuals whom I would like to thank for their support and advice, literary and otherwise, while writing this book. First and foremost I thank my best friend and partner, Michael Vincent Connelly, for his uncompromising friendship, patience, solidarity, tireless assistance, and unwavering faith in my abilities—without him I would never have been able to complete this project; Joseph Early and Sandra Rush, whose infinite patience, innumerable kindnesses, critical overview, and thoughtful consideration were not only proof of the deepest friendship, but equal to the best editorial advice; to Reni Santoni and Tracy Newman, without whose assistance and counsel at a time when I most needed it I would surely never have been able to complete these works; to Roberto

Poli, Ian Lindsay, Daniel Wnukowski, and Jonathan Tsay, each of whom is a magnificent pianist and a consummate artist who should be a household name soon enough; to the distinguished Liszt scholar and pianist Kenneth Hamilton; to Michael York and Hugh Downs, both experienced authors whose support has been unwavering and who have also shown tremendous patience in reading and critiquing my manuscripts; to Margarita Fyodorova, who taught me all about intonation and much more; to Rick Bechard, whose eye and ear as a documentary filmmaker were invaluable as he helped me to reconsider both style and narrative, which I can only hope find in these volumes a writer who does them justice; to Gordon and Emily Jones, Julie Marsden, and others in the extended Putney School family, for their encouragement, kindness, and help; and to my editor at Amadeus, Bernadette Malavarca, and also copyeditor Angela Buckley, for their invariably right critical assessment and editorial observations.

Finally, to those who are no longer with us, I extend my gratitude in ways that I can only hope will be borne aloft on the wings of angels. From these individuals I learned much of what I know of music. Among them are Constance Keene, a great pianist who was my teacher and mentor for nearly thirty years; Michel Block, likewise among the great pianists of the twentieth century, whose extraordinary musical savoir faire, supported by his personal gentility, provided a continual source of knowledge and enrichment; James Landrum Fessenden, a brilliant philosopher and musician whose early death was a blow to all who knew him and whose generosity of spirit and willingness to share his phenomenally authoritative knowledge of any number of disciplines, from aesthetics to epistemology and psychoanalysis, have proven invaluable; and to both Claudio Arrau and Ernst Levy, each of whom taught me more about Beethoven and music making, in my few brief encounters with them, than most could have done in a lifetime.

—John Bell Young
Putney, Vermont
February 2008

Introduction

In this volume, it is my objective to survey great music from a personal perspective, just as anyone would. Whatever I can convey of my ideas about listening, though informed by analytical scrutiny and historical data, will not be enslaved by technical analysis. While academia continues to do its job in the classroom, pointing out the idiosyncratic formalities of this or that composition as it teaches students to more effectively recognize compositional strategies, I prefer to do what I can to bring music to life in a kind of dialectical dance. These slim volumes for Amadeus Press, then, are part musical analysis and part interpretation, but, above all, a personal appreciation. My work here is not intended to be, nor should it be construed as, a work of scholarship.

Nowhere will I presume that the reader will be following my musical observations, or the accompanying CD, with a score in hand. So often when we listen to music, things seem to fly off the page of the score or from the hands of the performer in ways that strike us as inexplicably new and exciting, as if we had just heard the piece for the first time. Perhaps that's just how it should be. In any case, in attempting to put myself in the shoes of listeners, both those who are familiar with this music and even those who may not be, I will do my best to bring them into the dynamic fold of the music as it reveals itself. And while there are certainly advantages to examining the score, there is also much to be said for letting your ears do what they do best when you trust your instincts: listening!

Though I presume that readers will have a minimal knowledge of the vocabulary of music, or access to information that would explain such things as meter, rhythm, note values, bar lines, and the array of Italian-language tempo and dynamic markings, I will nevertheless attempt to demystify some of the larger issues pertaining to musical experience.

To this end I will evaluate, describe, and convey as much as possible about compositional process and interpretation. Thus as we begin this survey of Liszt's music, let's have a look at a few basic technical concepts, albeit nothing too intimidating.

Let's start with the notion of tonality. What does that really mean? If you think of a work of tonal music—that is, music that depends for its very existence on the organization of its parts into tonal regions, or keys, and their relationships—as a kind of solar system, with planets, asteroids, meteors, light, and infinite space, you will also have to conclude that somewhere or other there lurks a sun, too. And just about everything in this musically construed solar system orbits around that sun.

What I am getting at here is that the home key is akin to the sun, and its purpose similar. The home (tonic) key is a kind of sonorous landscape that gives sanctuary to the all the parts of a composition and that welcomes them home when they drift away or go off on their own into other keys. This tonal center exerts its own kind of gravitational pull, too. Everything in its sphere of influence moves inexorably toward it, and we experience this movement as fulfilling. The moment we return to the home key we sense a certain satisfaction, as if things were meant to return there all along. In turn, the parts of the composition—its rhythmically organized notes and motives—are irradiated by the heat of this musical sun, which not only envelops its progeny in its ever-present rays, but assures them of its power and permanence.

I would like to propose changing the paradigm for the discussion and analysis of music. For those who may not be so comfortable with technical terminology, no matter how fundamental or arcane, have no fear. While I could certainly refer to the home key of any tonal composition as the *tonic*, or to its closest relations as the *dominant*, *subdominant*, and *mediant* (the common terminology of harmonic analysis), I prefer, for the purposes of this book, to deal less with technical matters and instead raise more experiential questions: How is it possible for our ears to recognize a musical event as it happens in real time, and once we do, how do we determine its significance? Are some events more significant than others? And while it's all well and good to identify the various elements of a musical composition by name, what use is that kind of exercise for listeners who are unable to do so?

To appreciate and recognize significant compositional events as they occur, it may prove more productive to focus our attention on both the rhythmic and melodic progression of the work at hand. In other words, what we ought to ask ourselves as listeners is not to which key this or that chord belongs, or how the imposition of a Schenker graph would illuminate both form and harmonic structure, but something even more essential: Where are things—by which I mean melodies and rhythms—going, where did they come from in the first place, and how did they get there? By what visceral or aural means can listeners untrained in the vocabulary and complexes of music find their way home and back?

Think of it this way: all of us know very well our own homes. We know how they are laid out, where the furniture is, where we've made open space or indifferently created clutter. If we are particularly well organized, we may even know what lurks in the darkest recesses of every closet and behind the rakes and shovels in the garage. During a power failure, when everything is thrown into total darkness, we can find our way around, though the gentle illumination of a small candle, even in a familiar place, would be welcome and might prevent us from stumbling over the unforeseen.

If this sounds like the stuff of an Alfred Hitchcock thriller, it is indeed possible to make an analogy to the genre of the mystery novel. Just as Agatha Christie keeps us on our toes in anticipation of whodunit, providing clues alluded to by the heroes and villains of her texts, so does a composer proffer information, albeit in musical categories. These musical clues are called *motives*, which are the musical equivalent to literary characters.

We can easily recognize a motive, no matter how brief, by its rhythm, pitch organization, melody, or mood. The eminently familiar first four notes of Beethoven's Fifth Symphony, for example, form the driving motive of that work. All great composers are resourceful, never failing to organize the elements of their music clearly and intelligibly so as to allow us to follow their train of thought. They will provide signposts and goals, and as the work progresses, they will develop, vary, and elaborate their materials. Eventually the home key—our sun—will reappear on the compositional horizon and beckon us back to the familiar place where the journey began.

Savvy listeners will strive to cultivate their listening habits and inscribe themselves within the musical activity, as if they themselves were creating the music as it unfolds in time. To a certain extent listeners, as real-time participants who process the stream of sound, are doing just that. In art music complexity—that is, its myriad parts, rhythms, harmonies, and, not least, the interrelationships of these—is something not to be feared, but to be embraced. Listeners untrained in the context of analysis who finds themselves unable to name this or that compositional form, harmony, or technical particle should not be intimidated. Not everyone is a professional musician, or can be, and woe be unto a society replete with professionals but wanting for amateurs. In the final analysis, having an encyclopedic knowledge of music in all its details is unnecessary and unimportant for the nonprofessional music lover, because when it gets right down to it, what really matters is listening with an open mind and an open heart. To this end we can, each and every one of us, decipher musical form, whether in its smallest incarnation (the motive), which is nothing more than a fragment of a larger picture, or in its largest array, be it a fugue or a sonata. Repetition is vital to understanding the architecture of musical form.

Thus it is not without purpose, both structural and pragmatic, that the laws of composition have traditionally demanded, de rigueur, the repetition of whole sections. As we listen to music, patterns emerge as we follow its myriad melodies, fascinating rhythms, and changing harmonies, which embed themselves in our perception and memory. Our ears become accustomed to these patterns. Through this process, with the composer's help, the destiny of each motive evolves before our eyes (or should I say, our ears) and "catches fire on form," to cite the German philosopher and critic Theodor W. Adorno. Finally, a motive takes its place within the larger formal context it informs, influences, and ultimately helps to create.

If my methodology in this small volume appears somewhat eclectic, it is. Liszt wrote hundreds of piano works, and although all of them deserve lavish attention, alas, it is impossible to treat them equally in these few pages. My decision to focus on certain works is in part a consequence of my own studies and experience as a pianist. All of the works I've selected here have at one time or another played a significant part in my repertoire, both onstage and off, and also in my teaching. Because of the sheer volume of Liszt's output, and the limits imposed by publication, a more elaborate discussion is impossible. Fortunately, those readers who want to explore the music of Liszt even further have a both a friend and a guide in Alan Walker, whose magnificent three-volume, 1,800-page-plus biography remains a broad and authoritative survey of Liszt's music in all genres. Thus I recommend Walker's august work for a more comprehensive look at the music. And for a volume devoted to piano playing and performance practice in Liszt's day, Kevin Hamilton's rigorous study is a treasure.

It is my hope to introduce to newcomers to Liszt's music something other than just another brush with a popular Hungarian Rhapsody or such evergreens as the lyrically abundant if overplayed *Liebestraum*, or that old conservatory favorite, "Un sospiro." Those works, known to just about anyone who has seen an old movie or listened to radio, certainly represent Liszt but by no means define him. On the contrary, Liszt's music demonstrates tremendous variety and growth, just as it should in light of his imaginative genius and unusually long career. Thus the importance of the massive, though hardly popular, *Années de pèlerinage* (Years of Pilgrimage—see Chapter 3 for a complete survey of this work) to Liszt's development cannot be underestimated. Given the history of its composition and decades-long gestation in its final and earlier forms, its inclusion for discussion here is indispensable. What's more, as the *Années* can be interpreted as a kind of musical autobiography and thus reflective of its composer's vibrant but constantly changing aesthetic philosophy, it behooves us to examine each of the individual works it comprises.

Like other major composers who enjoyed relatively long careers, Liszt's creative period is generally divided into three periods: early, middle, and late. While his youthful works may have lacked substance and poetry, instead favoring bravado and audacity, they also pointed the way to the music of his later years. It is no accident that Liszt so often recomposed his early music, lending it greater breadth and depth as he matured.

This was also the period that has come to be known as his *Glanzeit*, or "glory days," when he was better known throughout Europe as a celebrated virtuoso pianist than as a composer. After retiring from the concert stage in 1843, he devoted himself almost entirely to composition and teaching. After his fiftieth birthday in 1861, he began to intuit his days were limited; indeed, age fifty in those days was well beyond middle age. For a while, as we shall see, he abandoned the idea of a musical career altogether, planting himself in a monastery, where he took the minor orders of the Catholic Church. But he could not resist the call or the urge to begin composing again, though now his aesthetic agenda had changed. Gone were the parlor tricks of his youth and the blustery rhetoric of his early maturity, in favor of a new kind of music, at once lean, harmonically adventurous and conflicted, and austere.

To help with this analysis, the glossary accompanying this text provides succinct definitions of theoretical terminology. Just think of each of these musical terms as representing a significant change or event of some sort: invariably, such changes and events refer to harmony, rhythm, dynamics, and melody.

Music is an adventure. If I succeed in cultivating in readers a renewed curiosity about its many recesses and shadows, rivulets and canyons, all the better. Certainly I make no claims to be right or wrong; after all, the most rigorous harmonic and formal analyses are probably better served by theorists and scholars whose work is more useful to each other than to nonexpert music lovers. The latter, after all, are those who simply strive to become as intimate with musical experience as they can without becoming scientists. It is to those *amateurs de la musique* that I dedicate this volume and who I hope will find within its pages something of value.

Franz Liszt: An Overview

In one of the more sentimental, if unintentionally hilarious, films of all time, *Song of Love*, a radiant Katharine Hepburn, in the role of Clara Schumann, finds herself at a soirée with her husband, Robert (played by Robert Wagner), and a perfectly effervescent Franz Liszt (portrayed with sardonic relish by Henry Daniell). On the heels of Liszt's particularly fiery, even excessively machismo, performance of his paraphrase of Schumann's celebrated song "Widmung" (which was itself a testimony of Robert's love for Clara), Madame Schumann takes a seat at the piano and plays the same thing, though in a manner a thousand times more affecting and tender. The following exchange ensues, and though it is a screenwriter's fantasy, it encapsulates amusingly and succinctly Liszt's unfortunate and undeserved reputation as a superficial fake, an image that outlived him for decades:

Liszt: Why don't you play something?

Clara: I'd love to, Franz. You are a brilliant artist, Franz. I envy you. I wish I had the power to translate the commonplace into such stupendous experience. Once in a while, though, a little moment comes along, which seems to defy such translation. You know what I mean, Franz. The littlest things, the wonder and the magic, two hearts that speak perhaps one to another, the unimportant things. Love, Franz, as it is. No illusions, no storms at sea, no guilt, no glitter, not the rustle of silk and the diamond garter, Franz. Just love . . . unadorned . . . Or do you know what I mean?

Princess: Whoa! She insulted you!

Liszt: She did much worse than insult me, my dear: she *described* me!

While those words strike us today as the height of kitsch, there was indeed a time when Franz Liszt was condemned, even among professional musicians, as the shallow person this admittedly fictitious version of Clara Schumann saw fit to describe.

Charlatan to some, visionary to others, Liszt had celebrity as his calling card. As one of the first major international stars to avail himself of photography, still a relatively new technology in the mid-nineteenth century, Liszt himself was as much responsible for his persona as were the burgeoning media of his day.

But the complexity of the man was at least equal to that of the musician. Composer, bon vivant, pianist, showman, raconteur—Franz Liszt was all of these. Since his death in 1886, a legion of biographers have paid homage to his musical as well as entrepreneurial genius and have unraveled his life in a manner that would make even Pavarotti blush. He has inspired philosophers, too, not the least of them Vladimir Jankélévitch, who devoted an entire tome to the concept of virtuosity, as if Liszt alone had invented it.

The passagework to this point provides a telling example of why Liszt, even at the height of his powers as a romantic-era hero and celebrity, was so terribly misunderstood. To his opponents, such meandering in the household of technical bravado was little more than meaningless drivel. His opponents—and there were many, not the least of whom was Brahms—disdained the programmatic and theatrical elements of Liszt's vision, advocating instead purer musical values that eschewed technical display, at least for its own sake, altogether.

As we shall see, the theatrical dimensions of music, left over, perhaps, from opera, were indeed indigenous to Liszt's pianistic and musical vocabulary. But they were also relevant to his reinvention of piano music as something greater than the sum of its parts. Those who disparaged his music throughout his life—and the enemy camp consistently failed to acknowledge the profound changes that his compositional style underwent over nearly six decades—were put off by the admittedly shallow showpieces of his youth, as much as they were by the showman Liszt himself. Liszt was never quite able to shake that image after retiring, when still a young man, from the concert state in 1842.

While it is true that a number of his youthful compositions were superficial, especially those that served largely to show off his technical arsenal to delight a rapt audience, there is no dearth of his work that was substantive. Even so, Liszt had the presence of mind to interpret his early works as experimental. To that end he often returned to them more than once in his long career in order to reinvent, rewrite, or simply harvest them for use in his mature music.

Indeed, early virtuosic works such as the *Album d'un voyageur* (1838) or the *Études en douze exercises* (1825) would later inform the estimable compositions of his later years. He would refashion the former into the magniloquent *Années de pèlerinage* over the course of some twelve years (fifty years, if you take into account the work's third book). Twenty-five years later, he brought into artistic focus the latter, fiendishly difficult, exercises, which we now know as the Transcendental Études.

It would have been an easy matter for Liszt to exploit his popularity as a pianist at a time when the idea of superstardom was just getting started. The commercial rewards alone would have been the envy of any number of his colleagues. Instead, he chose instead to abandon the concert platform altogether, save for the occasional charity benefit or private soirée, so as to concentrate on what really mattered to him: musical composition. A less gifted and sincere composer, especially one who commanded what, by most contemporary accounts, were extraordinary pianistic abilities, might well have gone on to write even more impossibly difficult music of dubious aesthetic merit. It was Liszt, after all, who invented and popularized the piano recital as we know it today, as a kind of theatrical ceremony in its own right. (Arthur Rubinstein once noted, with his customary humor, the similarities that a piano recital has to a wake, in that the performer, decked out in finery, sits before a long black box surrounded by flowers, as onlookers, some of them given to weeping, sit in respectful silence at an equally respectful distance; for that we have Liszt to thank.)

Franz Liszt was born in Raiding, Hungary, on October 22, 1811. At that time, Raiding was part of the Hapsburg Empire but since 1922 has been in Austria's Burgenland. His father, Adam Liszt, was an amateur musician—a cellist—and a functionary at the celebrated estate of the Esterházys. Because of Hungary's proximity to Austria, Liszt's native tongue was in fact German, not Hungarian. Indeed, Liszt's attempt to learn Hungarian later in life came to nothing; by that time even his German had become rusty, and he had long since adopted French as his principal language.

While his musical descendant Béla Bartók, whose cultural identity was never in dispute as Liszt's often was, spoke of Liszt's musical output as essentially French in character, Liszt himself would have disagreed. Throughout his life he felt an affinity with Hungary and to this end, through his music and charitable assistance, he drew as much public attention and goodwill as he possibly could to that country.

Liszt's musical proclivities became apparent by age seven, but not until October 1820, when he had reached the ripe old age of nine, did his musical potential, at least as a pianist, became a matter of public speculation. His first public performance of note was one that he shared with a well-known violinist of the day, Baron von Praun; Liszt played a juvenile work of his own, as well as a concerto by Ferdinand Ries. Some months later, in November 1820, Adam Liszt arranged another event for the prodigious boy, who he was convinced would become another Mozart. Taking advantage of his connections, Adam Liszt curried the favor of Count Michael Esterházy, whose palace in Pressburg became the site of Liszt's next concert, attended by a wealthy coterie of Hungarian aristocrats. Liszt senior secured a modest annual stipend from these august individuals. Though these funds were hardly rose to the level of support his son needed, Liszt the elder nevertheless requested and was granted a leave of absence, sold his property, and took off for Vienna with his family.

The year was 1822, and Vienna was still the musical capital of the world. Beethoven was still very much alive and kicking, as was the far less well-known Schubert. Chopin had not yet left Poland for Paris, and Robert Schumann was barely a teenager. Here Liszt would have every opportunity to become a first-class musician, and to that end he took lessons with Carl Czerny, whose authoritarian manner bothered Liszt as a child but whom he sincerely revered for the rest of his life.

But the Liszts' days in Vienna were few. A year later, in 1823, they moved again, this time to Paris. It was Adam's idea, and indeed his strongest wish, to win his son a place at the Conservatoire, which in those days was the most prestigious institution of its kind in the world. But the French being French, the Conservatoire's Italian music director, the composer Cherubini, declined the request, because Liszt was, well—a foreigner!

But in Paris, which became the soon-to-be-itinerant musician's geographical mistress for years to come, Liszt made a name for himself, first as a child prodigy and then as a dynamic, devilishly handsome virtuoso. His association with the piano firm Erard, whose owner, Sebastian Erard, developed the double-escapement mechanism, did much to support his ambitions, as did the innumerable piano compositions that became his calling card. However, these works—among them the rather sketchy Études in Twelve Exercises, Variations on a Theme of Rossini, Op.2, and the two works titled *Allegro di bravura*, Op. 4—amounted to much more than the fanciful, if adolescent, machinations of a fascinating if not yet mature talent. As a child, Liszt could not claim a gift for composition on the level of Mozart, Chopin, or even Mendelssohn. That did not seem to bother the public, whose express satisfaction led to handsome fees in France and abroad. He was only thirteen years old when he first visited England, for example, where he enchanted audiences left and right.

Following the death of his father from typhoid fever in 1827—a traumatic event for Liszt who, up until then, had so completely depended on the man's advice, support, and devotion—his professional and personal life slowed to a crawl. He became depressed, frequently battled illness, and turned to the mysteries of Catholicism for comfort. He also moved into a flat with his mother, living there for more than five years, before taking up his own digs in 1833. So reticent had he become in this period of his life that *Le corsair*, a leading Paris journal, published his obituary in October 1828. In fact he had taken a job teaching at a private school for girls on the rue de Clichy.

Only two years later, in 1830, the intellectual pursuits and theories of Paris's leading intellectuals, among them Victor Hugo, Felicité de Lamennais, and Alphonse de Lamartine, stimulated his imagination and rescued him from the oblivion his life might have become. But Paris in 1830 had again become a hotbed for revolution, when King Charles X, determined to obliterate the constitutional monarchy born of the earlier French Revolution in favor of the long-defunct absolutism of Marie Antoinette's day, was defeated. Charles's attempt to turn back the clock was met with fierce resistance by just about everyone, including students and laborers who rioted and protested around the clock and without mercy. What a pity, then, that the new regime, led by King Louis-Philippe, established even more draconian laws that compelled many of the city's leading artists and intellectuals to flee. As we shall see, Liszt himself, in part owing to such circumstances, departed Paris in December 1830 for Geneva, where he aligned himself with the Saint-Simonists and their movement, which advocated a kind of Christian socialism grounded in the teachings of Christ but libertarian in its outlook.

Before leaving Paris, Liszt became acquainted, about this time, with the City of Light's newest star, Frédéric Chopin (1810–1849), and the odd, manlike female writer long associated with Chopin, George Sand. He also met, for the first time, Felix Mendelssohn. Chopin's compositional genius was already apparent, but his sharp tongue was not, at least not immediately. Privately, Chopin demeaned Liszt as a pianist who couldn't hold a candle to Kalkbrenner. Elsewhere, Mendelssohn disparaged Liszt as a dilettante.

He also became friendly with Hector Berlioz, whose radical, harmonically adventurous music he not only admired but valued as a kind of romantic role model for his own burgeoning aesthetics; and he befriended the painter Delacroix, whose portrait of Chopin is perhaps the most famous of all. Liszt's image would later be immortalized by any number of artists, but Henri Lehmann's elegant painting, now at the Musée Carnavalet in Paris, stands out even today as the most memorable.

But it was most certainly the wildly popular violinist Niccolò Paganini (1782–1840) who most inspired Liszt. After hearing Paganini perform in 1832 at a charity event organized for the benefit of Parisian cholera victims. Liszt swore to himself that he would become to the piano what Paganini was to the violin: an uninhibited creature of fantasy capable of giving expression to any musical idea, no matter how complex or seemingly impossible. But it is also not unreasonable to presume that Liszt had something else in mind besides music, as a condition of his ambition—namely, to duplicate Paganini's ability to manipulate the public to his advantage.

For the concertgoer, Paganini was not human, but a wizard who used the violin to bewitch anyone within earshot. Adulation became for Paganini a condition of his virtuosity. A delicate bond tied him to his listeners and consequently engendered his fame. Liszt's ambitions were enormous, and his materialistic yearnings, amplified by his modest if wholly dependent childhood, convinced him that Paganini's path was the one to emulate. How could he have known that he would not only do that, but surpass the violinist by light-years in both performance and compositional categories?

That said, it would be an exaggeration to suggest that material success was at the top of Liszt's wish list, or that he desired it above musical creation. The Belgian critic and musicologist François-Joseph Fétis's (1784–1871) lectures on the future of music likewise stimulated his imagination, particularly Fétis's theories of omnitonality and omnirhythms. Perhaps a measure of Liszt's overall largesse and tolerant disposition is evident in his appreciation of Fétis, who loathed the music of Berlioz, whereas Liszt unabashedly admired it.

What Liszt lacked in formal education—he was, throughout his life, both embarrassed and regretful that he we never properly schooled—he made up for in intellectual and artistic integrity. He was a voluminous reader of poetry, fiction, theology, and philosophy. And his musical vision not only embraced the relationship between music and literature—and also theater—but served to make of that vision a reality.

Liszt's encounter in 1832 with the Countess Marie d'Agoult, a married woman, would change his life. An earlier love affair in 1828 with his piano student Caroline de Saint-Cricq, who at seventeen was only a year his senior, was likely not consummated, but its dissolution following her mother's death led Liszt into serious depression. Ever the ladies' man, he took up soon after with the wealthy Adèle de Laprunarède, another married woman.

The later affair with d'Agoult was born of experience and a certain maturity, and though it did not last all that long, either (they lived together for five years, from 1834 to 1839, before finally separating), its effect on Liszt personally and professionally was significant. For one thing, their liaison produced three children, including Cosima, who later married Richard Wagner. The other two, Daniel and Blandine, died young. With Marie at his side, Liszt traveled throughout Europe as a touring virtuoso, and the subsequent, acrimonious dissolution of their relationship led to innumerable difficulties for the composer, far too many to elaborate in this nonbiography.

With his quotidian relationship with Marie d'Agoult at an end, Liszt continued to pursue his glamorous concert career until 1847, performing throughout Europe and Russia and making frequent visits to Turkey. Satisfied that he had done all he could as a concert pianist, he turned his attention exclusively to composition, though the occasional charity concert was hardly beneath him. In 1842, after taking a position in Weimar as a Kapellmeister, he entered into a romantic and professional liaison with yet another married woman, Princess Carolyne von Sayn-Wittgenstein, who would remain absolutely devoted to him until he died. They planned to marry, but as we shall see, it was not to be.

The attractions of Weimar must have been great, as Liszt decided to settle there permanently in 1848. It was in Weimar that Liszt's talents as a composer, a conductor, and even a concert promoter flourished His intention to bring to Weimar what was then contemporary music, though not entirely fulfilled, was unique; he conducted the premiere of Wagner's *Lohengrin* in 1850. And it was in Weimar, too, that he composed the B Minor Sonata, a dozen symphonic poems (including his most celebrated orchestral work, *Les préludes*), and the two piano concertos.

This was also the period of the advanced version of *Années de pèlerinage* and so much other music that gave voice to his rhetorical and literary sensibility. For Liszt, musical aesthetics could not or need not be solely determinative, relying on conveying meaning from within the work itself. Rather, he saw and attempted to realize the potential of theater and literature to endow music with aesthetic dimensions unavailable to any other art form. To this end his bold experiments with musical narratives correspond to those of the romantic novel, for example.

Just as the French philosopher and semiologist Roland Barthes would opine a century later, music, like a book, yields itself most fully when approached dialectically by those who aim to master it its content; music demands a certain kind of participation from listeners, who can invest themselves emotionally, often cathartically, in musical experience, in much the same way they can enter into the mind and soul of a character in a book. In other words, Liszt's music was meant to be played from both sides, as it were, rather than just made an object of exogenous contemplation for others, or merely diminished to the executable duty of the pianist. In Liszt's music, the performer enters into an implicit affair with the listener.

Italy called out its siren song to Liszt on his fiftieth birthday, and he relocated to Rome in 1861. But as well connected as he was with the Catholic Church, and despite his friendship with Pope Pius IX, he was dealt another blow when he learned he could not marry Princess Carolyne, thanks to unavoidable familial and financial conflicts on her side. And in Rome, the religious thoughts that had haunted Liszt in the late 1820s, after his father's death and the loss of his first love, Caroline de Saint-Cricq, returned. He again began to seriously contemplate a life in the service of the Catholic Church. To this end, he took the minor orders of the church in 1865.

Liszt was widely known as a gentle and giving man, who rarely had a harsh word for anyone, at least publicly. He had a delicious sense of humor, the abundant evidence for which is drawn from the accounts of his contemporaries and especially his students. He cut an imposing figure with his chiseled features, coal-black eyes, and long white hair lightly dusting the black cassock he cultivated, from his religious internment forward, as a kind of uniform. Generous to a fault, he taught without fee, taking in students from all over the world, even America. But underneath the polite facade was a man who had been broken and hurt. This hurt did not disable or cripple him personally or professionally—he was far too resolute and impassioned for that—but it affected him in ways that his music now began to reflect. The unexpected deaths of his son Daniel in 1859 and his daughter Blandine in 1862 affected him deeply. A near-estrangement with his daughter Cosima left him disappointed and uneasy, especially after Cosima's conversion, in advance of her marriage to Wagner, from the Catholic faith to Protestantism.

What's more, while some of the music of his youth remained very much on the public radar, especially his operatic and song transcriptions, the works of his advanced age fell on largely deaf ears, not the least of which belonged to critics. The audiences who once adulated him as a pianist and even as a composer of glittering virtuoso fare now expressed bewilderment, dismissing his music as the creepy machinations of an old buzzard. The gloomy patina and acerbic isolationism that pervades so much of his late music—the *Bagatelle sans tonalité* (Bagatelle without Tonality), *Nuages gris, La lugubre gondola*, and even the haunting F-sharp Impromptu featured on the accompanying disc here—may be a consequence of his maturity and a considerate aesthetic point of view, but it was also not born in a vacuum.

There had always been a halo of sexual allure around the charismatic Liszt, too; in his youth, his mastery of the piano—itself an emblem of domesticity that had long since been culturally reified as a feminine instrument, to the extent that it represented a certain stability that could best be conquered and tamed by a man—he was akin to a modern-day rock star. After all, in concert he made women swoon and compelled men, or at least male musicians, to want to be like him. That the music of his old age, for all its interiority and expressive angst, proved incapable engendering any such reaction or energy must have hurt him on some level, as it would any composer whose work goes unappreciated. But it certainly didn't disillusion him, as the music's appeal spoke to a more rarefied species of exaltation and ecstasy.

Liszt's musical output is enormous and his contribution to musical composition so profound that it is no wonder that Alan Walker wrote three five-hundred-page volumes to elaborate it all. Even so, the stark austerity of the composer's late music, which extolled fragmentary motivic configurations and pungent harmonic inventions, looked forward to Scriabin, Schoenberg, and dodecaphony. Liszt expanded the vocabulary and the limits of sonority as he compelled pianists to move beyond boundaries that, until he came along, they did not even know they had. Having reinvented virtuosity for posterity, he moved on in his musical compositions to reimagine harmony in a way that anticipated the development of minimalism nearly a century later.

While it is true, as we have observed, that critics dismissed his late music or bashed his youthful compositions as superficial, no one could afford to ignore Liszt in his lifetime. University after university showered him with honorary doctorates, awards, and citations, and the aristocracy and the church bestowed him with one exotically named honor after the other. He was the proud owner of orders, memberships, pensions, crosses, noble titles, gold medals, citizenships, and more. He accepted them all graciously, and was grateful for the recognition, but never let any of it go to his head.

In July 1886 Liszt caught fever, which was complicated by travel from Frankfurt to Bayreuth. He had promised his daughter Cosima, now a widow, that he would attend the Wagner Festival, which she ran. But illness quickly overtook him, as his coughing turned to bloody expectoration and his fever to delirium. His biographer Lina Ramann's chilling account of Cosima's neglect of her father in favor of her business with the festival, as well as reports of a possible accidental injection of camphor or morphine into his heart, suggest that his demises was deliberately accelerated. Whatever the case, his age was advanced, particularly in the nineteenth century, in an era without antibiotics or the medical methodologies that might have been able to sustain him a bit longer today. Certainly, his long career—much longer than that of any other major composer of his day or the previous century—rather overshadows what certainly would have been the inevitable ravages of the body he endured. On July 31, 1886, Liszt died at home in the company of his doctors. Cosima and her family had a dinner engagement, and though they had visited him earlier in the day, they were not willing to wait for the inevitable end.

Though it can certainly be argued that there is a Liszt performance tradition—or better yet, traditions—it is not within the scope of this book to elaborate anything of the kind. Rather, my objective is to examine the music in a way that the nonexpert listener can understand, from the inside, as it were. Rather than argue the validity of this or that performance practice, thus extolling a performer or performance—though at times, as we have already observed, something of that, too, will be necessary—my objective is to evaluate the compositional motors, aesthetic dimensions, and compositional vocabulary that drive and ignite Liszt's abundantly fascinating music. While there are any number of those who advocate a return to some vague, even ersatz manner of playing that was supposedly common to nineteenth-century players, as if there was some reified, monolithic formula for music making that had no use or interest in musical values, I prefer to let the music speak for itself.

There is certainly some truth to the protestations of those who continue to cling with conviction to the idea that the pianists of Liszt's day embraced such practices wholesale. Among other things, these idiosyncratic practices included playing one hand slightly ahead or behind the other in an effort to more effectively segregate a melody from accompaniment or delineate it within the context of the prevailing harmony; adding octave doublings, elaborate ornaments, notes, or whole passages to a work; altering harmonies and rhythms in order to dazzle listeners with technical bravura and colorist effects; and as Kevin Hamilton rightly points out in *After the Golden Age*, preluding, too, became a practice wherein a pianist publicly improvised, just in advance of performing a given work, a slew of chords, arpeggios, and the like so as to acclimatize an audience to a key or a style. (The pianist Josef Hoffmann often did just that throughout his long career, which lasted well into the 1950s.)

Such practices, while common in the nineteenth and early twentieth centuries, were not universally approved or accepted by every performer. But in spite of that, there are certain music lovers who, in their sincere zeal to embrace some idea of authentic romanticism, see such arcane practices (which beg for relevance) for emulation today, for no other reason than it was something that some pianists did more than a hundred years ago. Ironically, these diehard devotees and protagonists for an authentic performance practice have reified precisely what they seek to enervate. Today we listen with rather different ears than our ancestors did, and we have the benefit of hindsight, experience, and a comparative lexicon of music going back more than four hundred years. We are not our ancestors, and any attempt to blindly re-create a performance practice absent its historical context strikes me as ludicrous.

Rather, a synthesis of styles and approaches, judiciously adjudicated and thoughtfully considered—for what these may bring to or take away from musical experience—and a responsible interpretation (that is, one that takes seriously the composer's intentions, as notated) ought to prevail. Though it is true enough that the notes in a score are only a point of departure for interpretation and not the stuff of uncompromising demand, it is equally true that centuries of compositional procedures inform composers' judgment of just how best to provide their intentions in writing. It is also true that music was never intended, by Liszt any great composer, to be pigeonholed as something formulaic, rigid, or mechanical.

And yet, while hardly perfect, notation is hardly a system that merits systematic abuse and sentimental exaggeration in favor of a performer's ego. Its entire purpose is to codify, with specificity, a composer's intentions with regard to pitch material, dynamics, metrical configuration, form, structure, counterpoint, and voice leading. Rhythm (which cannot be confused for meter) and its innumerable subtleties (not the least of which is the *inégale* in baroque music, for example, or rubato) has remained the most elusive constituent of the art, resisting written codification. And on this point, the sentimentalists cum authenticists are on to something.

As we shall see, Liszt's reputation as a composer of superficial compositions is ill deserved and more often than not is the fault of pianists, largely, who prefer to emphasize the technical dimensions of his works. In so doing, they misinterpret the very idea of technique, confusing it with the physiological mechanics of piano playing. But technique is a far broader concept that embraces musical values, not the least of which are articulation, balance, contrast, color, musical tension, and the recognition and conveyance of metrical and formal organization.

Though some of Liszt's earliest and immature compositions deserve to be called acrobatic—an array of fiendishly arranged notes devoid of meaning, purpose, or substance whose sole agenda is to allow an itinerant virtuoso to entertain and impress an audience—the overwhelming majority of his compositions are anything but. Given the pure volume of his output, a detailed overall critique of all his piano music would be impossible in these pages. Thus I have limited this survey to works that, in my view, will provide readers with a representative but substantial swath of his piano music that embodies the best of Liszt as a man, as a spirit, and as a composer. If my choices seem eclectic, it is because these are also works that I have played, performed, and taught frequently for many years; thus I cannot entirely claim impartiality in my selection.

In this volume I take a look at the entire *Années de pèlerinage*, a work that is central to Liszt's creative output. In many ways it is his musical autobiography, in that its composition and its conceptual development were the products of his inquisitive imagination for more than fifty years. From the earliest versions (1830s) of some of the individual works that populate it, to the final touches he put on the last of them in the 1870s, they articulate the aesthetic principles he cultivated as a young man and developed more fully later in life. The *Années de pèlerinage*—at turns programmatic, religious, and philosophical—merits special attention.

As there is not enough room to look into all of Liszt's piano music, I've included only a representative swath. In addition to the B Minor Sonata, which is vital to any discussion of Liszt, I've selected individual works from the *Harmonies poétiques et religieuses,* the Hungarian Rhapsodies, the Transcendental Études, and the operatic paraphrases. Additionally, I've turned my attention to a few of his late masterpieces, which so profoundly influenced musical composition in the twentieth century, from Ravel and Scriabin to Bartók and Messiaen.

The Sonata in B Minor, S. 178

CD Track 1

Were you to ask any professional pianist to name only one work in the piano literature that deserves the description "apotheosis," odds are the answer would be Liszt's Sonata in B Minor (or simply, "the Liszt sonata," as most pianists refer to it). While its challenges, both interpretive and technical, are innumerable, no professional concert pianists would ever dare to ignore it. To master this enormous, nearly thirty-minute-long work requires an enormous battery of skills as well as musical maturity, without which its glittering array of rapid scales, granitic chords, punishing octaves, and elaborate arpeggios can easily degenerate into little more than vapid display.

Performances of this magniloquent evergreen are akin to a virus: they seem to proliferate, and nowhere more so than in conservatory practice rooms. For all its majesty, it has attained to a kind of ubiquitous presence on the concert stage, where its interpretation is often distinguished less by difference than by similarity. Fleet-fingered conservatory students, eager to prove their mettle, drag it into their graduation examinations and, if they're lucky, into the recording studio. Its litany of octaves and arpeggios supply ample opportunity for young piano lions to strut their wares. But the results, where dedication to its musical dimensions is compromised, are usually the same: fast, loud, and belligerent.

But as luck would have it, such bellicose bravado is anathema to seasoned and responsible musicians. Just as a house becomes a home, so does a thoughtful study of the Liszt sonata evolve over time into something both probative and intimate. It is a gold mine of compositional integrity and resources, which its greatest interpreters have taken time to explore in detail. It rewards those who have the patience to live with it and who are willing to explore critically, but without prejudice or preconception, its innumerable immanent relationships.

Among its greatest interpreters, the late Claudio Arrau extolled the work's autumnal grandeur, but not at the expense of its Catholic pretensions. In his hands it became a musical cathedral, wherein its litany of torrential arpeggios, double octaves, and omnipotent chorales, like flying buttresses, assured structural integrity. Arrau's interpretive investment was well rounded and uncompromising, in that he envisioned the work as a disembodied life form, whose journey from conception to annihilation relies on breath and heartbeat. Alfred Brendel, on the other hand, arrived at a wholly different conception, conveying much of the sonata's symphonic scale, rhythmic intensity, and orchestral breadth. From the Russian side, the polyphonically savvy Vladimir Sofronitsky, whose listening apparatus was so preternaturally acute as to differentiate and unravel its busy counterpoint with uncanny transparency, endowed the sonata with a kaleidoscopic viscosity and tensile elasticity that few pianists, before or since, have been able to duplicate. His fellow Russian, Lazar Berman, too, issued a stellar and exceptionally stimulating reading of the sonata, at once robust, fastidious, colorful, and regal.

There is also Ernst Levy's inspired, monumental, and wholly unique reading, which sees in the sonata the debt its composer owed to Beethoven. Levy's is an improvisatory performance that fearlessly exploits the work's radical contrasts as it extols its audacious conflicts and pungent dissonance. Alfred Cortot, too, brought his Gallic sensibility in to the work in a sweeping, goal-oriented, impassioned performance astonishing for its continuity. Finally, there is the case of Vladimir Horowitz. While his mannered, fussy, porcelain-doll reading (I refer to his famous 1930s recording) missed the point entirely, at least in compositional categories, it nevertheless amused and impressed everyone for the sheer reductionism, which converted Liszt's spiritual grandeur into so many now-you-see-it, now-you-don't parlor tricks. Even so, one can certainly argue, no matter what verdict his performance may lead to, that Horowitz had a firm grasp of the theatrical, dispatching the sonata with such diablerie as to charm anyone within ear range.

Liszt dedicated his Sonata in B Minor to Robert Schumann, a composer he sincerely admired. Some years earlier, Schumann had dedicated his own Fantasy in C Major to Liszt. But the Liszt sonata, unlike the Schumann fantasy, has had its share of detractors ever since its composition some 154 years ago. It has been vilified as little more than overblown bombast, an exercise in musical futility that at best spins out and varies a few nifty tunes ad infinitum. It has been dismissed as nothing more than the egotistical outpouring of a second-rate composer. Even those who should know better have sometimes been defeated by their own prejudices; a conductor friend of mine, an enormously gifted and brilliant individual, loathed the work so much that he would disparage it at every opportunity, opining that the only thing Liszt neglected to do was to set words to the famous grandioso theme. According to this conductor, those words should have been "Kiss me, I'm beautiful."

Liszt's ill-wishers, in defense of their position, often regurgitate the famous story that Brahms, upon hearing Liszt perform the Sonata in B Minor, promptly fell asleep, to the horror of everyone in the room. Though Brahms is reported to have shrugged off the incident, attributing it to fatigue rather than a deliberate, none-too-subtle critique, the pejorative residue engendered by the story survives to this day. That's unfortunate, as it has since become the stuff of a myth meant to demean Liszt at the expense of the sonata itself. It certainly was a story that sat well with Brahms's friend the influential critic Eduard Hanslick, whose outright disparagement was nearly as famous as the sonata itself.

Liszt gave birth to this, his magnum opus, in 1852 and continued to play midwife to its creation for another year. However, it was not until 1857 that his son-in-law, the pianist and conductor Hans von Bülow, gave its premiere. Its dedicatee, Schumann, never heard it; he had been committed to an insane asylum in 1854 and remained there until his death in 1856.

It was an unusually newsworthy decade, musically and otherwise. Giuseppe Verdi's *Il trovatore* had its premiere at La Scala, while in faraway America Harriet Beecher Stowe's *Uncle Tom's Cabin* saw the publication of its first edition. Elsewhere, the Russians and the Ottoman Empire battled it out in the Crimean War. And only two years after the sonata's premiere, Charles Darwin's controversial *Origin of Species* raised conservative eyebrows the world over.

There has been no dearth of analyses of the Sonata in B Minor, which has long since entered the repertoire and the public consciousness, given its numerous performances. Its thirty or so continuous minutes can put off listeners unwilling to sit through so much piano music at one go. Its significance in strictly compositional terms proceeds from the elegance and overall success of its form, which Liszt could not have claimed as unique. Both Schubert, in his "Wanderer" Fantasy, and Beethoven, in the finale of his Ninth Symphony, had successfully experimented with cyclical structure, which avails itself of sonata form while stringing together several movements into a single, uninterrupted musical stream.

What distinguishes this sonata from Schubert's "Wanderer" Fantasy is not the degree of uninterrupted continuity that links one movement to the next, but the fact that the entire work coalesces into what amounts to a *single* movement—in sonata form. With the finesse that only a composer of the greatest skill and musical cunning could have achieved, the major elements of sonata form—exposition, development, and recapitulation—take on a whole new meaning and are elaborated sequentially over time. For example, the massive middle-section Andante is not so autonomous as it first appears; it relies entirely upon and also serves as a development for the motivic material presented in the first third of the sonata. In other words, it is a sonata within a sonata, as if two forms were unfolding in time simultaneously. From this perspective, the Sonata in B Minor fulfills both its function and its destiny as immanent critique; it is a work that observes itself in action and comments along the way, in compositional terms, on its own progress and efficacy.

This brings us to a dimension of the sonata that is perhaps even more remarkable than its formal architecture. Holding this sprawling mass together is a compositional strategy, to wit, *thematic transformation*. As I noted in my analysis of the "Wanderer" Fantasy in another of my books in this series, *Schubert: A Survey of His Symphonic, Piano, and Chamber*

Music, thematic transformation is a process whereby themes and motivic material are significantly altered with each appearance and made subject to harmonic and rhythmic enhancements in varying contexts. From this compositional perspective, themes attain to autonomy to such a degree as to become nearly unrecognizable whenever they rear their heads. The entire Liszt sonata, for example, relies on only four motivic fragments (which might best be described as abbreviated themes), which are alternately embellished, varied, prolonged, and concealed.

I would be remiss to ignore, however, the extramusical dimensions that inform the Sonata in B Minor, which are nearly as robust as its compositional constituents. While any number of literary sources might have informed Liszt's imagination as he wrote it, the music itself has fallen victim to fanciful interpretations that hold it hostage to specific works of literature or genres. Among these are Milton's *Paradise Lost* and the biblical tale of Adam and Eve. Even the myth of Hero and Leander, which some believe informs the program of a later work, the Ballade in B Minor, has been proffered as a candidate for the sonata's inspiration. The Faust legend, too, has gained considerable currency as its ideational genesis. So abundant is the hyperbole over the Liszt sonata that even the story of Genesis itself—of God and the devil, creation and annihilation, sin and redemption—has established it, in the popular imagination, as something akin to the Sistine Chapel of piano sonatas.

Liszt's spiritual anxieties, deeply held Catholic convictions, and genuine faith in a good and omnipotent God are well documented. Thus, whatever the source of the sonata's multivalent themes and motives, it is hardly a stretch to attribute their inspired formation to Liszt's religious values. As we shall see, the various motives that inform the sonata from its outset are telltale tags whose thematic construction suggests something beyond the litany of notes and rhythms that spawn them.

The first of these, which I will refer to as motive A, is a slow, descending Gypsy scale whose ambiguous tonality seems far removed from the key of B minor. It articulates the sonata's seven-measure introduction. Marked "lento assai," its color is dark, even lugubrious, and its assignment to the piano's bass register enhances its prescient character. Indeed, the sonata ushers itself into existence on a quarter-rest, emerging from silence, but then alights on three G-naturals played in unison. The mood, murky and uncertain, hardly anticipates the vigorous Allegro energico that follows.

That the piece literally begins with silence is itself significant for performance and goes directly to the aforementioned issue of theatricality. How does a pianist effectively convey the function of that silence so as to avoid imparting to the very first notes, which occur on the second (weak) beat of the bar, the blunter feeling of a downbeat? Though this detail may, to the lay listener, appear to be unimportant, it is in fact crucial. The disposition of strong and weak beats, and their relationship to each other, is highly significant in the Liszt sonata, and the savvy and aesthetically responsible pianist should know that. The punctuation of silence with off-beats not only disturbs the rhythmic status quo, throwing the meter off, it casts a pall over all that is to come as it sets up the sonata's tenuous atmosphere. These jarring, interruptive off-beats must be perceived as disrupting silence; they are the first gurgles as the sonata-behemoth comes to life, the first utterance of an organism that, in the first few bars, is evolving out of the "chthonic muck," to cite Camille Paglia.

The ensuing six bars, moving from 4/4 time to an anxious alla breve, establish the primacy of a belligerent new motive. This simple figure, though grand, comprises a consecutive onslaught of octaves in disjunct motion, which terminate in every other bar with a descending triplet. Let's refer to this as motive B. But now the stakes have been raised as the motive bursts forth *fortissimo*, defines itself in an iambic dotted rhythm, and soars into the piano's upper register. Its character, though determined and pugnacious in its first incarnation, will soon enough become the basis for innumerable guises.

The bass register plays host yet again to the next motivic fragment, which reveals itself in only two measures itself a whole-step higher. We'll call this motive C. It is an insistent stream of five repeated D-naturals, which terminate with a flourish of two sixteenths and a chromatic descent of two eighth-notes, only to be repeated a whole-step higher just two bars later. It is no accident that this motive has been described as Mephistophelean: its rapid-fire staccato in such a dark register rings not portentous, but sinister.

With this, Liszt has introduced nearly every constituent of the sonata's extended motivic family, though one more important motive has yet to rear its head. On the heels of the imperious octaves and the diabolical motive B, a transitional passage emerges that bears no particular relation to the foregoing. Rather, it sets an uneasy mood with a sequence of arpeggios, each a distended configuration of rootless, derived dominants whose relationship to the tonic is no less ambiguous than the opening bars'. Modified by a sweeping crescendo from a ghostly *pianissimo* to a bloated *fortissimo*, it segues onto what could be interpreted as the exposition proper, where Liszt combines the motives thus far configured.

It is not unreasonable to suggest that the sonata, in a very real sense, begins here, as motives B and C butt heads in a torrential wave of sound marked "sempre forte ed agitato." The shadow of the A motive is barely discernable in the left hand in two groups of four sixteenths, if only by virtue of its reference to the introduction's overall teleology. As arpeggios tumble one over the other in febrile imitation, musical tension accumulates, culminating in a series of double octaves that, availing themselves of the B motive, thunder vigorously for ten bars in disjunct motion. Here, Liszt, like an imperious Zeus, hurls his thunderbolts to the sonata's terra firma, in the hope that something will catch fire and come to life. But the emergence of a new theme in D major, marked "grandioso" and unrelated to any of the motivic fragments established so far, comes as a surprise. It is a thickly harmonized chorale that conveys, with unmistakable authority, much of its composer's ardent Catholicism. It is as if, suddenly, out of chaos comes the voice of God.

This theme, a granitic chorale set as a profusion of major chords atop which a noble melody bellows forth in stepwise motion and minor thirds, has been singled out by scholars for its religious significance, owing to the likelihood that Liszt was at the very least inspired by the plainchant *Crux Fidelis.* As Alan Walker observes, Liszt turned to this chant in later works, including his oratorio *Saint Elisabeth* and in the *Via Cruces,* a choral work he penned only eight years before his death.

The insertion of this chorale, although it provides a brief but interpretively deceptive respite from the thorny technical challenges thus far, is problematic for the pianist. Liszt is specific in his demand that it be played *fortississimo*, a dynamic marking he uses only one other time in the course of the sonata, at the grand climax of the Andante. Its dynamic ferocity, therefore, competes with what is to come and requires careful adjudication. The chordal configurations, while thick, are exceptionally rich and majestic; any treatment that would make of them a hard and brittle display would serve only to defeat their translucent Brahmin purpose. They must, as it were, shimmer, their inner constituents rendered with a certain vibrancy. To effect this, Claudio Arrau recommended an approach he learned from his teacher Martin Krause, a student of Liszt. He suggested to imagine each of these chords as if they were arpeggiated but gave a stern warning to the pianist to avoid actually rolling them. Thus no one ought to arpeggiate the chords per se but should only lightly think of them as such, with a view towards separating the individual pitches by microseconds, if that. The idea, then, is not to break them, but to focus attention on the balance of their interior voices.

Whatever the case, the role this chorale will play in the rest of the work is estimable. As it hemorrhages into the next passage, the once bellicose C motive returns, morphing into a coy and tender melodic strand in the soprano voice. With its melancholy stream of repeated notes and periodic *grupetti*, its guise is wholly Italianate and, like so much of Liszt's music, owes its design and its character to operatic recitative.

The B and C motives join forces for the rest of the first movement, bubbling over into a scherzando vivamente, a glittering array of rotating sixteenths that spins an elaborate web around the B motive. The C motive follows, now emboldened within a militaristic onslaught of octaves and chords en route to an extended transitional recitative. This, too, emerges from the B motive, but this time it is recast as a serpentine melisma that moves headlong and without pause into the Andante sostenuto. Here Liszt again asserts his essential Catholicism in yet another placid chorale, this time in F-sharp major and loosely based on the B motive.

In keeping with the overall state of calm, the C motive resurfaces in the faintest *pianississimo*, now an ethereal ghost of its original incarnation. Without warning, the grandioso theme reestablishes itself in the lower registers and flirts with the B motive. The mood is as grand as it is somber; a passionate, even improvisatory survey of the extreme ranges of the keyboard, awash in octaves and chords, culminates in a climax that many interpreters have seen fit to convey as the sonata's most significant. The erotic disposition of this passage is evident enough as it heaves its way forward with cumulative determination; the accompanying chords in the left hand, syncopated on weak beats as the climax approaches. An ethereal spray of ascending scales drifts upward from the bass to the treble, as if to sanctify the proceedings, before reversing its trajectory in the spirit of tender consolation.

The movement closes with a lingering, sad, yet somehow austere cadence that is remarkable for its simplicity. The C motive, again transformed into an ardent and rhapsodic paean, again predominates here in a series of consecutive sighs, which swell and diminish, like long breaths, in abbreviated crescendos and decrescendos every three bars. The murky Gypsy scale of the sonata's opening reappears for eight bars, drawing the Andante sostenuto to a quiescent but mysterious close.

Suddenly, the key changes to B-flat minor and a new but surprising transformation of the thematic material is under way. Liszt reinvents the B and C motives as a fugato. The texture is sparse, the mood menacing; if his intent was indeed to convey something of the diabolical, he succeeds brilliantly. With few exceptions, a staccato sign modifies virtually every note, as if the idea of detachment had itself become a virtue. The B motive, not to be outdone or shaken off, is subjected to inversion; it is literally turned upside down.

The principal material of the exposition returns soon enough, though the passage in double octaves is now replaced by fireworks of a different kind, a più mosso that lavishes attention on a series of arpeggios that encompass the lower and upper registers. A wickedly acrobatic but thrilling bit of virtuosic rhetoric ensues in the form of a breathtaking stringendo in advance of the chorale's return in a manner somewhat less strident than we remember it. Now the mood is more subdued, the dynamic marking reduced to *mezzo forte*, and the repeated chords of the exposition spread out as slow-moving arpeggios in the left hand.

The sonata's elaborate coda brings all the elements together in a virtuosic fury. Going from fast to faster (presto to prestissimo), Liszt toys with octaves, transforming the mysterious Gypsy scale of the opening into a forceful statement that crashes headlong into a virtual confrontation of the B and C themes. The endearing grandioso chorale makes its final appearance, once again reclaiming its omnipotent status in triple *forte*. Indeed, as Alan Walker astutely observes, Liszt's original intention, in his sketches for the sonata, was to combine the new chorale theme with the B motive (Allegro energico, thus rendering it somewhat less autonomous). Had Liszt settled on such a configuration, the chorale, no longer able to consolidate itself as new thematic material, would have lost much of its power, here as well as in the exposition.

At this point, Liszt's ill-deserved reputation as a pompous thunderer evaporates as the Andante sostenuto rears its head, and every one of the motivic strands is humbled in *pianissimo*. The work ends in an ethereal chordal progression—A minor, F major, and finally, the tonic B minor—in what can only be deemed an unmistakable musical vision of heaven.

Of particular interpretive importance in the opening measures of the Liszt sonata are the indices of articulation, or wedges, that modify the opening octaves. While tradition has long held that these wedges (as opposed to dots) should be interpreted to mean that the octaves are to be played extremely short, as if they were pizzicato, the truth may lie elsewhere.

Certain contemporary pianists, particularly the Russians, have accepted this approach, convinced Liszt's intention, in placing the wedges where he did, was to eviscerate the tones of any breadth and resonance whatsoever.

The advocates of this point of view insist that even the pointed fugato of the sonata's final movement demands precisely such mechanical adjudication. Even Alan Walker, in describing the fugato, opines that "the passage must be drained of human feeling. It is the denial of self-expression, the suppression of 'interpretation,' that reveals the diabolical qualities lurking within. The colder and drier the performance the more remorseless it will sound."

Of course, we all know what Mr. Walker is getting at: that these presumably diabolical passages in the Liszt sonata ought to, at the very least, come off as austere and relentless. But his choice of the terms *colder* and *drier* to describe musical affect is unfortunate, in that they convey nothing of what is involved either in the body of the composition or in the interpretive obligations of the performer. The responsible performer, on the contrary, will follow Liszt's explicit instructions, which he codifies plainly with specific dynamics and articulation markings: Hairpin crescendos, staccato dots, and a litany of deftly accentuated, differentiated wedges and lighter accents atop downbeats all inform this sonata, and this passage in particular.

To point up any diablerie in its most conventional sense—as a force of evil or ruthlessness—the pianist needs only to emphasize the harmonic contradictions that inform the passage. These are embedded within every harmonic construction, no matter how lean and no matter whether configured as chords or even as a single continuous line: dissonance and its resolution (or lack thereof) provide plenty of opportunity for the pianist to explore the expressive potential of the given material. Certainly, nothing speaks more persuasively in defense of diablerie than the gritty, grinding oppositions posed by dissonance within a vertical construction or even over time.

In case anyone should forget, the creatures—be they demons or shadows or fallen angels—that populated and inspired Liszt's imagination were in every instance metaphorical projections of oh-so-human models. It was hardly a robot that Liszt set out to represent—the very idea would have been anathema to him—but the strengths, the weaknesses, the inherent good or evil that mingle, to lesser or greater degrees, in every individual. It was Dante's *Inferno* and its fictional coterie of shadows and demons—all projections of human qualities or spiritual aspirations born of humanity—that inspired Liszt from early on.

The Sonata in B Minor is hardly an occasion where out of the blue, Liszt has merely abandoned either his literary inspiration or his spiritual idealism in order to suppress interpretation and extol the value of remorselessness. On the contrary, Liszt was preoccupied with issues of redemption and transcendence generally, and in this work specifically.

There are those whose point of view parts ways with some of the Russian pianists'. Take Claudio Arrau and Ernst Levy, for example, whose interpretations, though wildly different, agreed on at least one thing: and that is the character of the opening octaves. For these artists, these introductory bars were not merely an evocation of sinister forces, but something that ought be interpreted in a wider dynamic, rhythmic, and even extramusical context. Indeed, the mystery of the passage relies on breathing, allowing the rests to frame the halting, newborn exhalation that signals the beginnings of life. Cutting off the reverberant sound of each octave too soon fails to respect affective inflection in favor of legitimizing something machine-like and mechanical.

If there is anything demonic about this passage, it is that it has a human face; these ambiguous, unharmonized octaves on the remote sixth degree of the scale suggest emancipation as they materialize out of nothingness (the rests). They give voice to the darkness of the low registration and throw a frame around the ominous mystery of the descending Gypsy scale that follows. Thus, what is required to convey their mystery is neither a pitchfork nor a stick, but the lungs of the Brahmin; the notes hardly need to be strangled of their breadth and potential, but discreetly separated one tone from another. The rests in between them already ensure as much without additional help. When considered—and delivered—from this perspective, resonance is not compromised.

Arrau and Levy eschew any reading that would reinvent the sonata's introduction as something dry and devoid of vitality. Thus, to impose a clipped, severely shortened staccatissimo, in the interest of effecting a sinister atmosphere, serves only to compromise its richer potential and signification, pigeonholing interpretation into a narrow norm from which it cannot escape.

Années de pèlerinage *(Years of Pilgrimage), S. 160, S. 161, S. 162, S. 163*

The title *Années de pèlerinage* may appear to embody wanderlust. But it does not. Nothing about this work embraces, as does Schubert's song cycle *Winterreise*, the idea of alienation and loneliness. On the contrary, these twenty-six efflorescent, exceptionally varied works were composed in the spirit of personal fulfillment, curiosity, and camaraderie while Liszt set out to see Europe with Marie d'Agoult. Certainly, he loved to travel, but to dismiss the *Années* as program music or a musical travelogue would be to underestimate its overall aesthetic purpose, as well as its long-term relevance to its composer's spiritual ideology.

Liszt's particular brand of wanderlust was that of the spirit; it was not born of loneliness or pain or agony, but of his Catholic aspirations. Here was a fundamentally religious man who yearned to discover where his deep faith in God would lead him. While it is true that his travels as a touring pianist through Italy, Switzerland, and the rest of continental Europe with Marie d'Agoult over nine strenuous years provided him with at least one source of musical inspiration, these were, in the end, only a metaphor for *Années de pèlerinage*. In the end, Liszt's journey was a quest: for truth, beauty, and spiritual fulfillment in a powerful and beneficent God.

Inspired by art, poetry, and literature, Liszt, like so many people of his day, embraced the power of nature and what it had come to symbolize in post-Enlightenment Europe. Natural phenomena—rivers and streams, forests and flowers, moonlight and wind, for example—had acquired new significance in the early years of the nineteenth century.

Images of such bucolic reverie had become metaphors for evolution and progress, extolled by poets for their enduring power.

The *Années de pèlerinage* is central to Liszt's life and aesthetic sensibility and stands out as one of his greatest achievements. The individual works it comprises combine autobiography and engaged observation, personal confession and exorcism, optimism and critical forethought. Musically, their journey lasted some fifty years, and thus the work bears testimony to his development as a man and a musician.

The seeds of the *Années de pèlerinage* can be traced to 1832, when the Marquise Le Vayer paid tribute to the twenty-one-year-old Liszt, who was the guest of honor at his estate. Only ten years had passed since Liszt, on the arm of his father, first entered the City of Light. And here he was, his reputation as a virtuoso pianist already firmly established, being fêted by the rich and powerful.

In attendance was the Countess Marie d'Agoult, an heiress to a banking fortune and a serious-minded young lady whose angular features and penetrating eyes would soon be amply captured by the painter Henri Lehmann. Lehmann's now celebrated portrait of the young Liszt, too, would inspire passion in young women across the continent.

But it was hardly a painting that was to become the national anthem of the all-consuming love affair that would eventually carry them off. The impressionable d'Agoult was already committed, in a marriage of convenience; her husband was a distinguished military man, the Count Charles d'Agoult. But Marie was capricious and manipulative. While professing her love and admiration for the count, to whom she had committed a dowry of some 300,000 francs, she had designs on Liszt. Within minutes of meeting him, her agenda was to become his mistress. Even the death of her six-year-old daughter from an inflammation of the brain failed to change her plans; if anything, this loss convinced her to throw herself into the arms of Europe's most famous maestro.

And that is precisely what she did. Two years later, Liszt and Marie had become the subject of scandal, their illicit affair having at once alienated and stimulated polite society in Paris. Having had enough of the gossip and the idle chatter, d'Agoult wrote a cold though respectful letter to her jilted husband, formally severing whatever ties she could short of a divorce. She then went on to join Liszt in Basel, Switzerland, where the first fruit of their affair, their daughter Blandine, was born only months later. It was the year 1835, and d'Agoult, perhaps less at ease than she cared to admit with the itinerant life of such a celebrated concert artist, resigned herself to her new role as his loyal companion, if not wife.

Together this distinguished pair, whose reputation preceded them, traveled throughout Switzerland and Italy, often in the company of a no-less-celebrated entourage. Their often raucous liaisons with the virago author George Sand and other democratically minded literati are well documented, while Liszt's concerts, perhaps more so than his music, enchanted those who heard him. Uncertain if and when they would ever be able to return to Paris in the midst of the scandal they had created, the couple's life together, while not exactly low-key, was played out in the fringes of urbanity. In 1837, only two years before Marie would return to Paris and to a family that had forgiven her indiscretion, she gave birth to another daughter, Francesca Gaetana Cosima, who later dropped the first two names in favor of the third, Cosima. Long after the affair between Liszt and Marie d'Agoult had sputtered, Cosima would marry the conductor and pianist, Hans von Bülow, and then Richard Wagner.

In this environment Liszt began to sketch his *Album d'un voyageur*, a collection of pieces inspired by the sights and sounds of Switzerland. He later elaborated on this suite of musical vignettes, completed in 1840, and fashioned them into the first book of *Années de pèlerinage*, which was published some fifteen years later in 1855. Still later he added two pieces, "Eglogue" and "Orage," before embarking on the second volume, inspired by his travels in Italy and published in 1858.

The *Années* might have stopped there, had it not been for Liszt's evolution as a composer. By 1867, when he began writing the third and most austere book of the *Années*, Liszt had already taken steps to fulfill his clerical ambitions. Nothing, not even music, could compromise his piety. To this end, in 1866 at age fifty-five, he assumed the four minor orders of the Roman Catholic Church. He had long since abandoned his itinerant life as a touring virtuoso in favor of what he came to view as more substantive issues.

In the nine pieces that constitute the expansive first book of the *Années*—called "Suisse"—Liszt offers musical tableaux inspired by the Swiss countryside and its folklore. Thus does he pay homage to the aesthetics of an earlier time, which valued the power and potential of nature. In "Au lac de Wallenstadt" and "Au bord d'une source," for example, he pays tribute to benign placidity of a lake, and glistening rivulets of a running brook; in "Pastorale," in "Vallée d'Obermann," and in "Le mal du pays," he paints mountains in tone; and in "Pastorale" and the gentle nocturne that is "Les cloches de Genève," he draws closer to the human dimensions of community and heritage. Yet each of these works, though evocative of natural phenomena, is not merely an organic doppelgänger or a bit of representative portraiture in sound; they are, both collectively and individually, an expression of Liszt's unshakeable faith in creation itself, and in the entity that informs it.

Even as it segued into romanticism, the classical era's preoccupation with landscape painting and poetry—itself a metaphor for evolution, growth, and change—continued to exert its influence. As if to disavow any confusion as to his aesthetic purpose, Liszt alludes in the titles of each work to poetic, artistic, or literary epigraphs inspired by Byron, Michelangelo, Senancour, and Schiller. While "Les cloches de Genève," for example, may at first suggest, both musically and by virtue of its title, the distant hush of bells in the Swiss landscape, it also points to the cathedral, and thus the temple of God, from which they emanate. Likewise, the unruffled, reflective waters of Lake Wallenstadt are nothing if not a symbol, in compositional categories, of contemplation.

In the second book, "Italie," Liszt dwells on rather different aesthetic objects, though his essential agenda—the moral and aesthetic philosophy, if you will, of the *Années de pèlerinage*—remains unchanged. Beauty remains the raison d'être, but certainly not for its own sake; in this book, the religious paintings, sculptures, and poetry of the Renaissance masters, Michelangelo, Salvator Rosa, Dante, and Petrarch, stand in for the nature symbolism of the earlier book.

The seven works of the *Années*' third and final book concern themselves with philosophical issues as much as with interpretive challenges. Here Liszt reinvents the very idea of virtuosity, sublimating the physicality of the work in favor of ascetic contemplation. It is no longer a mass of awkwardly configured note patterns that pose difficulty, as it once was in his youthful piano music, but affective expression itself that dares the pianist to maintain continuity. Continuity, harmonic evolution, tempo relationships, and sound itself join hands, as it were. Though the textures are leaner, and the notes fewer, the emblematic problems of musical interpretation have grown more complex and profound. They represent the culmination of a spiritual journey that looks back with distance and no little regret, perhaps, at the exigencies of everyday life. The titles no longer refer to landscapes, art, or literature, as they do in the first two volumes, but are awash in religious symbolism, even issues of life and death.

Liszt's preoccupation with a new, or at least newly inspired, spiritual aestheticism, codified in the last book of the *Années*, does not in the least foreclose his longings for as much in the previous two; the aesthetic trajectory of the set is a religious rite all by itself. Thus it is no coincidence that this last set begins with a prayer ("Angelus! Prière aux anges gardiens"), continues with three pieces (save for the brilliant, if symbolically spiritual "Les jeux d'eau à la Villa d'Este") that address, in tone, thoughts of the afterlife and ends with a nod to the Catholic mass ("Sursum corda" [Lift up your hearts]), where the priest enjoins his pious flock to take joy in their faith.

"Première année: Suisse" (First Year: Switzerland), S. 160

"Chapelle de Guillaume Tell" (William Tell's Chapel)

The fanciful if largely apocryphal story of William Tell, though based on fact, has long fueled Swiss mythology. It concerns the exploits of a skilled archer who, upon having insulted the effigy of a local political tyrant, is ordered to split an apple perched atop the head of his own son, with the promise that if he succeeds, he will be freed. Tell splits the apple, but then he levels yet more insults at his captor. The infuriated tyrant orders his execution, but Tell escapes and eventually tracks down and kills the tyrant.

The political tones of the William Tell legend are obvious, and though it would be difficult if not impossible to point to anything so specific in the musical text of "Chapelle de Guillaume Tell," one cannot help wondering if, in composing it, Liszt had in mind Beethoven's "Eroica" Symphony, itself a protest against the tyranny of Napoleon. Schiller wrote a play on the Tell subject as early as 1809, and more than a century later, Hitler, desperate that nothing would compromise his power, went to great lengths to disparage Schiller's work following an assassination attempt.

The work starts out optimistically enough in C major. Its mood is at once noble and pliant, its tenor abundant in *forte* and *fortissimo* in 4/4 time. Combining a march with a thick chorale, this opening has an emboldened determination that bespeaks it namesake's headstrong arrogance. This section is followed immediately by a long and vigorous passage of tremolos, which anxiously accompany a variant of the original chorale melody, now reduced to a melodic line in single notes.

The tremolo, an evocation of string vibrato, had special meaning for Liszt. The expressive potential of the tremolo demands a great deal from the performers, who, if they are savvy, will harvest it, whatever its length or function, for its harmonic content. There is more than one voice at work in the body of a Lisztian tremolo, as there is in this case, where a diminished chord is surveyed from afar. Diminished chords, in Liszt's musical vocabulary, are hardly superficial, but function as a means of prolonging tension; the immanent properties of these chords beg for resolution. The effect is that of a summons or voice from offstage, which becomes increasingly present as the chorale melody morphs into octaves only seven bars into the passage. Liszt intensifies the figure by double dotting it, an evocation of trumpets and horns.

"Au lac de Wallenstadt" (At the Lake of Wallenstadt)

Switzerland's picturesque Lake Walen, also known as Lake Wallenstadt, is surrounded by snow-peaked mountains and framed by what often appear, to visitors at least, to be perennially blue skies and crystalline air. It is also one of Switzerland's largest bodies of water, and a place inspiring for its serenity, as if its natural beauties were a metaphor for peace.

Liszt's musical portrait of this landscape codifies its placidity in the no-less-serene key of A-flat major. A rhythmically repetitive figure, awash in pedal points—that is, the insistent reiteration of a specific pitch—supports a spacious, evenly paced melody that evokes a flute or perhaps an alpenhorn. The melody expands into octaves before alighting on a delicate cadence that echoes a single pitch, the dominant E-flat, for several bars. As if to paint the undulating motion of the lake—the uncertainty of what lies under apparently placid surfaces—Liszt transforms the theme into a consecutive series of syncopes, only to enrich it again in dominant-quality chords en route to its quiescent conclusion.

"Pastorale"

Certainly, no one can argue that this lilting pastel does not evoke the natural beauties and sonorities of the countryside (the gentle hush of rivulets and streams, a shepherd's flute, distant horns, or bagpipes). But it is also evocative of a related musical form, the baroque pastorale, which set forth its principal melodic material in thirds and sixths as it hovered over an accompanying pedal point.

Like its ancestor, this pastorale sits comfortably in a meter of 12/8—twelve beats per bar—while its motivic material whispers comfortably within a fairly moderate, claustrophobically close set of pitches. Only twelve bars into the work, the patterns change; in the left hand the droning pedal points break into a yelp of open fifths in imitation of a bagpipe, while an urbane duet emerges in two voices in the right. The repetition of this material, which has thus far comprised only two basic themes, depends on dynamic variation to sustain its intensity. Liszt did not indicate *pianississimo* in the original manuscript; but in modifying the duet, on its second appearance, with two- and then three-bar long diminuendos, he implicitly asks for just that. The final two bars fade out gently with a stream of eighth-notes in the alto voice, while two open fifth—the tonic triad absent its third—echoes distantly in the bass.

But virtuosity is not merely a matter of how quickly and loudly pianists can play or even how deftly they can navigate the notes. The real virtuosos are pianist capable of drawing from music as complex as this an abundance of nuances, in the service of poetry.

"Au bord d'une source" (Beside a Spring)

One has to wonder why this shimmering confection, at once delicate and evocative, has inspired young piano lions to learn and perform it while still in conservatory. That only the most savvy and musically informed artists are capable of pulling it off betrays its real challenge, which is making of its abundance of notes, wide leaps, and hand crossings something delicate and poetic.

Among the works constituting the *Années de pèlerinage*, "Au bord d'une source" claims an unusual pedigree. In Rome, a young Claude Debussy, barely twenty-four and a somewhat befuddled recipient of the most prestigious composition prize in the world, the Prix de Rome, met and played for Liszt. But Liszt also played for Debussy, and it is perhaps no coincidence that it was "Au bord d'une source," a work whose impressionist or, more acutely, symbolic dimensions profoundly influenced the burgeoning French master.

The earlier version of "Au bord d'une source" (included in the *Album d'un voyageur*) is simpler, but not so elegant as its final realization. The textures in this final version are leaner. Here Liszt cultivates crystalline sonorities that rely on a continuous stream of sixteenth-notes, largely distributed in the alto register and punctuated by widely spaced eighth-notes in the bass and treble. The sixteenths are hardly a rigid accompaniment but form a contrapuntal melody all by themselves; though configured in what appear to be a single melodic strand, the pitch material implies, and contains within it, more than one melody. In this case, the first and fourth of each group of six sixteenths can be construed as the motivic germ of the one voice, while the other notes form a second voice. Only seventeen bars into the piece, Liszt migrates from A-flat major to E major, in an edgy harmonic relationship that serves to brighten the mood even more. He asks the player to indulge a velvety *pianissisimo* throughout, with few exceptions. This is a soft piece with discreet but vivid swells, thus fulfilling the dynamic context that Liszt so carefully indicates: leggiero, dolce, grazioso, and tranquillo. A return to A-flat major provides an opportunity to essentially reverse and elaborate the rolls played by the left and right hands. Here the left glistens with the arpeggiated sixteenth-note, while the right presses forward in a dialogue of slurred eighths.

Following a ghostly chromatic ascent in both hands to the upper regions of the keyboard, which alight on a transparent tremolando, the principal material resurfaces. But now the tension heightens en route to the only *fortissimo* climax in the entire work. Here, open fifths drone in succession in the bass below while the right gives voice to a swirl of rising arpeggios. The right hand alone articulates a succession of falling fifths in an even patter of sixteenths, leading once again to the aforementioned material of the earlier, all-too-brief E major section, where the sixteenths are given over to the left hand. A diminuendo anticipates a more vigorous presentation of the opening material before settling again into a diaphanous coda, its filigree as delicate as a spider's web, in triple *piano*.

"Orage" (Storm)

Although it is true that this unabashed bit of program music resists even the most thoughtful efforts of a seasoned musician, the fact remains that any pianist who fails to find musical value in the bellicose pages of "Orage" would be well advised to abandon Liszt altogether. How often has this work, corrupted and mangled by young players eager to show off what they naively mistake for technical acumen, been turned into an empty wasteland of pianistic tricks?

"Orage" is a reservoir of pianistic flourishes that combines roaring octaves and strident chordal profusion with double notes and arpeggios. Even so, underneath its array of ad libitum cadenzas, *fortissimos*, and pugnacious sforzandos—most of which occur within the context of its swift tempo (presto furioso)—there remains a narrative. Here Liszt paints a violent storm in the Swiss countryside, and to codify that image he engages a regime of dynamics and articulation that require fastidious adjudication. "Orage" celebrates the gesture, which is just another way of saying its motivic material. But in this work, gestures assume a heightened significance as balletic emblems of the extramusical idea they hope to convey, and they combine athleticism with affective nuance. Whatever the gesture—be it a throw of the hand over a wide distance, or a passage of rapid-fire octaves in crescendo—it can convey its musical purpose only by means of it immanent harmony and rhythm, and through the manner in which a pianist inflects these.

I am put in mind of a videotaped performance I encountered recently on the Internet, wherein an otherwise talented young pianist lost all control of "Orage," and imagined that only the physical, rather than musical, gesture mattered. Unfortunately, he was an undisciplined player who imagined that his constant grimacing and flailing about, while playing fistfuls of wrong notes and never taking his foot off the damper pedal, would suffice to convey the work's musical content. Certainly, his performance was theatrical. But in making his physical behavior the object of attention, rather than the music, he betrayed Liszt's intentions.

From the very opening, Liszt asks the pianist to pay attention. Hairpin crescendos modify the first salvo of six consecutive octaves in the second bar and do so again throughout the work in almost every measure. These crescendos require special care if they are to clarify the prevailing harmony. That's important for several reasons. For one thing, the imposition of a crescendo cannot be construed to mean that the figure it modifies must begin loudly and become louder still. On the contrary, each group (or gesture!) of octaves must recede considerably in volume—even to *piano*—in order to move forward and blossom effectively into a robust *forte* or *fortissimo*. The secret, if there is one, lies in the contrasts, which a savvy player will harvest for maximum effect. Even a work as overtly blustery as "Orage" offers plenty of opportunity for subtlety, at least for those who are willing to respect Liszt's instructions.

Another issue at work here is *harmonic rhythm*, which is the rate at which harmonies modulate and shift. In "Orage," that rate of change is relatively slow; the tonic is nearly always present, and where it isn't, dominant-quality chords or arpeggios flesh out the texture. Liszt's fondness for diminished chords gets the better of him in this work, which is not so harmonically adventurous as the rest of *Années*. In "Orage," musical tension is engendered by sweeping accelerandos, relentless *fortissimos*, and the manipulation of both for effect, rather than by any harmonic innovation. Thus the responsible pianist is obliged to look for opportunities where any event that goes astray of the status quo, be it an unusual dissonance or even a rest, rears its head.

A descending spiral of octaves spanning eight bars introduces "Orage." The principal theme (Presto furioso) is a long-legged affair of some ten bars, articulated in slurs over the first three beats and punctuated by staccatissimo chords; the last two bars of the figure are a slew of descending octaves in the right hand and violent dissonances in the left that a naive player might see fit to simply tack on to the end of the phrase, as if it were they were a meaningless afterthought rather than an intensification of what precedes them.

"Vallée d'Obermann" (Obermann's Valley)

Alongside the "Sonetto del Petrarca 104" and the "Dante" Sonata, "Vallée d'Obermann" is one of the more frequently programmed pieces in the *Années*. It's a dark, even spiritual work that is betrayed by the simplicity of its form. Liszt again relies on thematic transformation of its few fragmented motives as the principal means of fleshing it out.

In the early editions of the *Années*, Liszt cites a passage from a popular and critically acclaimed autobiographical novel of the early 1800s. Completed in 1803 in Switzerland by an obscure French novelist, Étienne Pivert de Senancour (1770–1846), "Obermann" is a collection of fictional letters by the novelist's protagonist, a sad and disillusioned man too lethargic to take action. He has resigned himself to living Switzerland's Jura mountain range, which becomes a musical metaphor for existential angst. The mood is one of abject melancholy, even hopelessness.

Thus, what Liszt attempts to evoke in "Vallée d'Obermann" is not so much a geographical location as much as it is an abstract vista of loneliness and isolation, inspired, as it were, by the view:

> What do I want? What am I? What may I demand of nature? . . . All cause is invisible, all effect misleading; every form changes, all time runs its course; . . . I feel, I exist only to exhaust myself in untamable desires, to drink deep of the allurement of a fantastic world, only to be finally vanquished by its sensuous illusion.
>
> All the ineffable sensibility, the charm, and the torment of our barren years; the vast consciousness of Nature, everywhere overwhelming, and everywhere unfathomable, universal love,

> indifference, ripe wisdom, sensuous ease, all that a mortal heart can contain of desire and profound sorrow, I felt them all, experienced them all on that memorable night; I have made an ominous stride towards the age of failing powers; I have consumed ten years of my life.

Inaugurating this work is the work's principal melody, an eight-bar-long plaintive wail in the tenor register in E minor that bespeaks the woes of isolation. The quiet accompanying chords move by in a sustained hush before the melody moves to a new position in right-hand treble. The contrapuntal texture is exceptionally thin; Liszt makes his point and sings the work's woes with eloquence and simplicity. This melody plaintively wails again when transformed, with limpid transparency, into an ethereal shadow of itself, but this time cast entirely in the treble voice and in the more hopeful key of C major. But things do not rest so easy; a blustering if thoroughly operatic recitative, awash in rapid tremolos in the left hand, gives way to a searing octave accompaniment.

As the tension heightens, Liszt indicates "agitato molto" and more than one hairpin crescendo before a registration confrontation of sorts; a brusque dialogue between the treble and bass ensues, punctuated by tremolo spurts and effected by a continuous crossing of the hands. An ardent, even languid reiteration of the principal theme follows, restoring the tempo to its original lento, though now in E major. The conclusion of "Vallée d'Obermann" gives voice, in octaves and arpeggiated chords, to an impassioned restatement of its lone theme, though now the texture is as thick and widely spaced as the opening was lean. As it draws to its bold *fortissimo* conclusion, its octaves ablaze, Byron's impassioned poem, which Liszt affixed to the score, comes into clearer, albeit metaphorical, view:

> Could I embody and unbosom now
> That which is most within me,—could I wreak
> My thoughts upon expression, and thus throw
> Soul, heart, mind, passions, feelings, strong or weak,
> All that I would have sought, and all I seek,
> Bear, know, feel, and yet breathe—into one word,
> And that one word were Lightning, I would speak;

> But as it is, I live and die unheard,
> With a most voiceless thought, sheathing it as a sword.

"Eglogue" (Eclogue)

The title of this delicate composition is rooted in literature. Though it may sound like a frothy dairy drink that ornaments one's dining table at Christmas, an eglogue (or eclogue) is a short classical poem on the subject of nature. It is, in effect, a pastorale. The genre is also known as *bucolic poetry.*

Liszt's "Eglogue" is all light and air, a cheerful and easygoing work without pretense; it evokes the famous statement, attributed to Freud, that sometimes a cigar is just a cigar. Indeed, there is nothing in the least melancholy or troubling rumbling beneath this work's pristine surface, no dark signifiers that point to anything particularly profound or even religious.

"Eglogue" opens in a most conventional manner, with the sparse configuration of distended chords in four-part harmony. Here, a single pitch, the dominant E-flat, prevails in the treble as a lone pedal point. Some seven bars into the work, a deftly articulated, marchlike stream of eighth-notes in whole tones and minor thirds drifts by blithely before the jaunty principal theme makes its first appearance some nineteen bars later. A filigree of triplets surfaces, distributed between the hands in a gentle haze, but not before the march theme makes a reappearance in the left hand. "Eglogue" doesn't end so much as it fades away.

"Le mal du pays" (Homesickness)

It seems only natural that "Le mal du pays" would find a suitable place in Liszt's European sojourn. Born Hungarian, raised a German, Liszt lived in France and Italy for much of his life; thus one can only wonder which land he pined for.

The answer to that question may not point to a particular geographical issue, but instead to Liszt's physical and spiritual cosmopolitanism. As early as 1835, Liszt held forth publicly that music ought be the common ground between secular and sacred ideals (an aesthetic philosophy, by the way, that the composer Alexander Scriabin embraced for different reasons more than sixty years later). This notion suggests that

Liszt's longing may be for another kind of home, an aesthetic paradise free from the exigencies of everyday life.

The solitary introduction to "Le mal du pays" wastes no time bespeaking its loneliness. A simple figure in four unaccompanied notes angles upward and then retreats in the next bar. An abbreviated chromatic scale ensues, descending beneath a haze of *pianissimo* triplets in the right hand. The melancholy principal theme, likewise a chromatic descent, and marked "Adagio dolente," surfaces some twenty bars into the work. It heralds a change of both of key and tempo—from E minor to G-sharp minor, and from 4/4 to the dulcet 6/8. Things heat up after a repetition of the material thus far, when an ardent agitato expands the registration and rings forte and appassionato before calming itself in the final measures, receding to the woeful melisma, now assigned to the bass, of the introduction.

"Les cloches de Genève" (The Bells of Geneva: Nocturne)

Though after significant revisions in the final version of "Les cloches de Genève" that set it apart from its first incarnation in the *Album d'un voyageur*—not the least of which is Liszt's determination to let the music speak for itself rather than rely on any perceived programmatic content—the work remains evocative of its title. In the earlier version, Liszt cites a bit of existential longing in Byron's *Childe Harold*, which he hoped would inspire the player to understand the compositions' musical ethos. "I live not in myself," Byron wrote, "but I become a portion of that around me."

From its opening bar, a plaintive musical strand made up of only an arpeggiated C-sharp minor triad, "Les cloches" weaves an exceptionally charming spell. Trancelike, the cloistral hush sets the stage; Liszt keeps us waiting five full bars before introducing the principal melody, a haunting ascent of eighth-notes. The dynamic moves from *pianissimo* to *pianississimo*, before the melody, now darkened, resumes in the tenor register. The evocation of bells vibrating in the distance gives way to a hardier, strongly accentuated motive accompanied below, in the middle voice, by pulsating waves of cascading sixteenths. Indeed, Liszt indicates that the accompanying figuration be played "quasi arpa"—like a harp. As this new musical material intensifies and thickens into ever-more-agitated arpeggios, ornamental roulades, and momentous octaves, the work cadences in an enormous triple *forte* in advance of the return of the opening bars in *pianissimo*.

This brings us to yet another dimension of Liszt's compositional strategy, to wit, a compositional device that has rarely if ever been discussed. I refer to the notion of *aural proximity*. I am hard pressed to think of a single major work of Liszt where something of this strategy is not put into play; certainly one finds it easily in late works such as *La lugubre gondola* and in the Sonata in B Minor. In "Les cloches de Genève," Liszt puts crescendos and tempo changes to work in such a way as to anticipate the imminent approach of a harmonic goal, or climax, and in so doing, he codifies geographical distance. In series of dovetailing crescendos, rhythmic diminution, and accelerandos, Liszt exploits the music's cumulative energy.

Perhaps there was something, after all, to Katharine Hepburn's portrayal of the composer Clara Schumann, whose contemptuous remarks, which I cited earlier as the invention of a 1940s screenwriter, pierced the romantic version of Liszt (played with sarcastic relish by Henry Daniell) through the heart. However, the purpose of such grandiose enlargement was never to impress, at least in Liszt's mature music, but was to bring the listener, body and soul, into the material fold of musical experience.

"Deuxième année: Italie" (Second Year: Italy), S. 161

"Sposalizio" (Marriage of the Virgin)

Liszt composed this, the first offering in the second book of the *Années*, in 1838. The then twenty-seven-year-old composer, already enamored of all things Italian, found inspiration in Italian art and literature, which at that time were relatively new to his otherwise voracious intellectual appetites.

The source of inspiration for "Sposalizio" was its eponym, a painting by Raphael. Its title is often translated as "The Marriage of the Virgin," and the work now hangs in the Pinacoteca di Brera in Milan. The painting evidently had such special significance for Liszt, who became enamored of it while visiting Milan, that he arranged with his publisher to have a drawing of it included on the title page of the score. This High Renaissance painting, which was commissioned in 1504 by the Albizzini family for the church of Saint Franceso of the Minorities in Umbria, depicts the marriage of Joseph to the Virgin Mary. Its own source of inspiration was a parable that Jacobus of Voragine made popular in his *Legenda Aurea,* a story that Liszt, given his religious proclivities, most likely knew.

As the painting's name unambiguously suggests, this work concerns the sanctification, through marriage, of the Virgin Mary. As legend has it, Mary was not committed to any man as the day of matrimony approached. To remedy this, a high priest gathers David's unmarried male descendants at the Temple of Jerusalem. Each has been instructed to bring with him a wooden rod. Once there, the Holy Spirit, who has made a surprise appearance, blesses Joseph and transforms his rod into an efflorescent blossom.

Raphael depicts the marriage of Mary and Joseph as a scene of contentment, with a landscape awash in soft reds and dulcet browns that calm the bright eggshell blue sky in the background. The symmetrical proportions of the various figures, human and inanimate, that populate the painting also lend it placidity. The wedding party stands admiringly on a public square, behind and to the side of Joseph and Mary, who are thrust into the center foreground. In the distance beyond, a polygonal stone temple rises beneficently, its wide porticoes and steps suggesting tradition and stability. The high priest presides over the sacred ceremony as onlookers gather 'round. Two of Mary's former suitors, appearing abandoned and disheartened, look on as Joseph places a ring on Mary's finger. In Joseph's hand is the aforementioned flowering staff, which is an emblem of his authority and his new stature as the Virgin Mary's one and only.

If Liszt desired to codify in music the compositional values of the painting, he succeeded. The musical work begins with a simple, unaccompanied diatonic figure played by the left hand. Its disjunct arrangement of ascending and descending intervals—major seconds and perfect fifths—inaugurates a four-bar phrase period that outlines the dominant. The very absence of chromaticism in this passage is striking; anxiety is banished in favor of a kind of wide-eyed innocence. It proceeds for two bars before an endearing new motivic fragment emerges in the right hand. Here the texture thickens as a light spray of falling and rising double thirds, imitative of horns and configured in a dotted rhythm, pipes in on the weak second beat of the bar. Its character is earnest and even a little elegiac. Though this figure is only a brief profusion of three beats, framed on either side by rests, its quizzical, even pious character is central to the work's aesthetic. By now the dominant is firmly established with a seventh chord and fortified by small hairpins (indicative as much of a diminuendo as they are a slight elongation of the metrical value), thus amplifying both the dynamic hush and a sense of breathy anticipation. Although the mood is serene, the continuous unfolding of thematic material in quarter-notes in 6/4 time lends a subtle prescience to the music that, in less skilled hands, might have been compromised.

Emboldened by octaves, the introduction is repeated, its quiet cadence colored by the tenuous presence of a doubled leading tone in the left hand and shaded harmonically by its mediant relation. The fermata that follows serves to heighten the tension as it distinguishes the introduction from what follows.

Like a distant apparition, the dynamic diminishes to triple *piano* while an arpeggiated aurora in the right hand evolves into a syncopated variant, played by the left hand, of the disjunct opening theme. Harmonically, things are not so much ambiguous as they are duplicitous. Liszt spells out a G-sharp major triad, whose hovering, irresolute status serves the function of a secondary dominant. Indeed, though it can be construed as the dominant of C-sharp major—the submediant of the tonic key of "Sposalizio," E major—it is also the enharmonic equivalent of an A-flat major triad, the dominant of D-flat major, a key associated with all things pastoral, and also a key through which the work migrates only a few bars later. The arpeggiated rotations of the right hand flirt with E minor and C major as the left hand angles upward in widely distended intervals, twice alighting, as if an effort to remember its roots, on an E-natural.

As the rotating arpeggios brighten under the influence of a long, twenty-one-bar crescendo, the left hand voices the work's introductory theme, its disjunct motion now cumulatively intensified in sequence. A pulsation of A-naturals at the crest of each wave of arpeggios enshrouds the harmony in a submissive, prayerful subdominant pedal. The overall effect is neither strident nor propulsive, but magisterial; Liszt has at once compressed and extended the progression of time. Suddenly, though imperceptibly, the meter changes from six to four beats per bar as the passage streams in powerful octaves toward a *fortissimo* cadence in E major.

Liszt again imposes a fermata to divide the sections, thus lending a formal layout akin to the sharply framed perspectives of Raphael's painting. Now the musical symbolism of the betrothal becomes apparent. Subjective an interpretation as it may be, imaginative ears might relate the disjunct quarter-note motive of the opening to the bustling individuals who form the wedding party, while the second motivic fragment—that earnest, somewhat pleading dotted figure—can be construed as symbolic of the betrothed Joseph and Mary. From this perspective, even the right hand's arpeggiated sequence, which led up to the cadence, sanctifies everything under its relentless hover and pedal points. It, too, takes on an aura of authority as it travels with relentless determination from quiescence to vigorous imposition; could this be Liszt's representation of Joseph's staff, itself a symbol of authority and masculine virility?

An eight-bar interlude restores the work to its quiet beginnings (marked "Andante quieto") and to 6/8 time, availing itself of both consequents of the principal thematic material. The key migrates to a remote region, G major, and opens onto a pious chorale. The restoration of triple *piano* is further intensified by the additional instructions to temper the dynamics, not the least of which is the muting of the piano strings with the una corda (left) pedal. He also modifies this new material with the marking "dolcissimo" (very tenderly) and a slight slowing of the tempo. More significant is the harmonic rhythm, which has nearly slowed to a crawl. Echoes of the diatonic opening theme ornament this chorale as it proceeds.

Distant bells are heard in the form of pairs of repeated octaves, which punctuate the chorale in the upper register. A proliferation of secondary dominants informs the destiny of the chorale, which only a few bars later flirts with the even more remote tonalities of C minor,

D-flat major, and B-flat major. Now the key reverts yet again to E major, and the chorale tune gives way to a chordal variant of the principal theme. The tempo and the harmonic rhythm both accelerate in a taut stringendo as the chords, now in quarter-note motion, press fervently forward to a forceful *fortissimo* climax. That the entire seven-bar passage so shrewdly exploits both dominant and secondary dominants makes the denouement especially powerful.

Here the chords debouche into a descending arpeggiation, which is nothing more than the opening theme in diminution. Liszt indicates a slight hastening of tempo: "Quasi allegretto mosso." While the left hand pulsates the diatonic figure in diminution, the right gives voice yet again to the chorale, now cast in the brighter E major and in a higher register. Now in tandem, both figures breeze by in a diaphanous *pianissimo.* A sudden crescendo swells to a blistering *fortissimo* as the chorale, its chordal constituents ablaze like trumpets, assumes an even more exalted position in the piano's uppermost register. The principal diatonic theme remains in diminution but is now belted out in a vigorous array of *fortissimo* octaves. Here Liszt, playing Jupiter, hurls thunderbolts once again.

The momentary downward drift of the key center, E major to E-flat major, and back again disorients the ear and culminates, some eighteen bars later, in the most powerful climax of the work, an imperial triple *forte* that virtually implodes, on the heels of a tumultuous descent in octaves, onto the betrothal motive. Here it becomes resplendent, every fiber of its motivic being now substantially expanded by chords and octaves. This presentation of the betrothal motive pays musical homage to the parental embodiment of the Almighty. To be sure, this is one of Liszt's grandest religious moments, an outburst of his spiritual sympathies in the form of secular music.

While the most ardent performance of this wholly inspired moment may seem at first like the stuff of some romantic *grande passion,* its aesthetic agenda remains of a quite different order. Here again the issue of Liszt's outward expression and inward feeling poses an enigma for his interpreters. The final climax of "Sposalizio" pits sincerity—that is, spiritual contemplation and inward intensity—against exogenous and superficial explosive expression. The passion and fiery intensity must proceed from the inside of the harmonies and dynamics that modify them, as it were, and as if the harmony itself has become rhythm. What goes on *between* the notes in a passage such as this will inform its transcendent character, as well as the efficacy of the performance itself. The organlike quality of its lush chords demands an engaged listening apparatus capable of hearing the pulsations swell and diminish in stasis despite the fact that, on the piano, sound can only diminish.

The coda unfolds after a lengthy pause, heralded by the imposition of a fermata. The pious tag of the betrothal motive breathes tenderly before hemorrhaging into a recall of the chorale, which is now played quietly by the left hand, in a single voice and in the tenor register. Above, the principal motive unfolds fluidly in diminution, now a hushed pastel of lightly falling arpeggios. As Sposalizio draws to a close, Liszt revisits the pious chorale, now a shadow of its former self in barely audible *pianissimo* E major chords. The work drifts away in a triple *piano*, the tempo likewise withdrawn into the embrace of a solemn adagio.

"Il penseroso"(The Thinker)

"Better not wake me! Better to be made of stone, and not to see or feel, as long as there is shame and suffering on this earth! Speak softly and do not wake me!" These rich words, which preside over the tomb of Lorenzo de' Medici in Florence, were an inspiration to both Michelangelo, whose famous statue *Il penseroso* (The Thinker) contemplates that very tomb, and to Liszt himself. Though brief, this dark, brooding work held special significance for its composer; Liszt had wanted it played at his funeral, but that wish remained unfulfilled.

"Il penseroso" begins darkly in the piano's tenor and bass registers, where the right hand gives voice to a grim and insistent dotted-eighth-note pedal point that evokes the tolling of a bell. The mood is rendered all the more somber by the key, C-sharp minor. Only eight bars later the pedal point shifts upward by a minor third to G-natural and yet again to a B-flat. Open fifths contribute to the uneasiness of the harmonic environment as they likewise pulsate in dotted rhythms. The texture thins to a single descending line in the bass, before moving on to a grim procession of C-sharp minor and A minor triads astride a relentless oscillation of eighth-notes in the bass. Swelling from *piano* to an enriched sforzando on an F major chord, the left hand moves chromatically southward. Here Liszt restores the C-sharp minor triad as the chromatic fall is taken over by the alto register. There is something monolithic about these measures, as they sulk downward with Wagnerian intensity.

In the penultimate measures, Liszt pits C-sharp minor against its Neapolitan neighbor, a D major triad giving way to a particularly ruminative and pungent dissonance. The funereal conclusion is at once stark and hopeless, as three low C-sharps, separated by quarter-rests, suggest the final vision of a coffin being lowered as the last bits of consecrated soil are shoveled atop it.

"Canzonetta del Salvator Rosa" (Canzonetta of Salvator Rosa)

This spirited if jaunty march is in some respects a portrait of a portrait. The Italian baroque painter and poet Salvator Rosa (1615–1673) was a virtual doppelgänger of Liszt; indeed, even a cursory examination of Rosa's self-portrait, which now hangs in the National Gallery in London, bears an uncanny physical resemblance to the composer as a young man. The long face, the aquiline nose, the high brow, and the long mane radiate, just as in Henri Lehmann's famous painting of Liszt, the qualities of an exceptionally charismatic individual.

But it was Rosa's poetry that inspired this cheerful work with a bit of braggadocio. "Though I move frequently from place to place, but I can never change the object of my desire. My burning love will always be the same, and I, too, will always be the same." The tune itself suggests as much. It is a spirited and confident ditty, of sorts, that thrusts itself forward in a distinctly articulated dotted rhythm. It sets out as a single unaccompanied melody before picking up steam and harmonization only two bars later. Expanding into the treble, the figure engorges itself on fatter chords that move away from and then back again to the work's bright tonic of A major.

A brief middle section introduces canonic imitation as its capital, giving way to an affective dialogue between the bass and treble. This subdued refrain is plaintive and gently chided by breathy syncopes in the middle register. A return to the original theme follows a two-bar cadence in F-sharp major that sets the opening theme quiescently in the registrational stratosphere. The opening theme returns and segues some eighteen bars later into a *fortissimo* punctuation of tonic and dominant chords. The canonic treatment of a fragment of the opening theme draws the work to a deceptive cadence on the tonic, only to be reprimanded, in the final two bars, with a *fortissimo* restatement of the same motive. Three determined chords, again arguing on behalf of the tonic and the dominant, provide a definitive closing tag.

"Sonetti del Petrarca" (The Petrarch Sonnets)

If there is a single centerpiece of the second book of the *Années de pèlerinage*, it is certainly the three Petrarch Sonnets, nos. 47, 104, and 123. Liszt's consecutive organization of these works in the midst of his Italian sojourn is no accident, as a literary thread links them one to the other: the sonnets of the Renaissance poet and humanist Francesco Petrarch (1304–1374). Of the 366 inventions that populate Petrarch's magnum opus, *Il canzoniere*, a collection of some 366 verses penned over a period of forty years, some 317 are sonnets. These include the three that Liszt set them to music, first as songs and then as loose transcriptions for solo piano.

It may be that Liszt intuited something of himself in Petrarch, who, like the composer, weathered with aplomb his celebrity status as an intellectual in an era where such an achievement, in the absence of mass media, was particularly hard earned and unusual. While possible similarities with the Italian poet in matters of artistic philosophy and public status may have fueled Liszt's ambitions, it was something else about Petrarch's ardent poetry that inspired him—an idea that would have been irresistible to any hot-blooded romantic, no matter his métier: and that idea was, of course, love.

Indeed, nearly all of the poems in the *Canzoniere* are devoted to, or concern Petrarch's unrequited love for, the mysterious beauty Laura, a married woman who captivated the poet's heart and imagination. Laura, it seems, was most likely Laura de Noves, the wife of Count Hugues de Sade, was a distant ancestor of the infamous Marquis de Sade. Though Petrarch first encountered Laura at the Church of St. Claire in Avignon, France, she declined his affections, and the two had little contact.

Liszt likely admired Petrarch's restraint and chivalry as much as he did his poetry, and perhaps, through musical composition, he attempted to emulate such sublimation of sentiment. Even so, that restraint came with a price, and that price was anguish. Though Petrarch codified in poetry the agony of an unattainable love that would never experience consummation, it was only after Laura's death that his melancholy began to diminish.

The Petrarch sonnets enjoyed a somewhat complicated history. While in Italy with Marie d'Agoult in the year 1838, Liszt waxed prolific. It was a period of exceptional productivity that gave way to compositional experimentation. For the most part, and not surprisingly, the piano was the conduit of his abundant ideas. In that year alone, Liszt penned his first versions of the Transcendental Études, the Paganini Études, the Italian book of the *Années*, and hundreds of other works.

Even so, it was another genre—the lied, or song—that preceded the phenomenal industry of his musical adventurism in these works. Petrarch's endearing poetry, with its rich use of Italian vernacular and its autumnal message, compelled Liszt to set each of these three sonnets for high tenor voice with piano accompaniment. Though no one can say whether he was dissatisfied with the results—though that strikes me as unlikely—one thing is certain: he intuited the songs' abstract potential as autonomous piano music.

For Liszt a new version of an existing work became a cause for celebration; given his cultivated ear and his unparalleled sense of fantasy, it would be a gross understatement to say that he merely revised or transcribed his own music, or anyone else's for that matter. On the contrary, the relationship of his later reworkings from their progenitors—is based not so much on similarity as on difference. From this perspective, the solo piano versions of the Petrarch sonnets are not vapid reductions of an earlier work, but are rendered as an entirely new and independent species of composition. Thus, while the Petrarch song settings may share a great deal of thematic material in common with their pianistic cousins, including a philosophical point of view by virtue of the texts that inspired them all, they part company in conceptual categories. Indeed, save for their easily recognizable themes, the piano works have evolved into elaborately wrought yet austere fantasies. In abandoning words in favor of abstract ideas, Liszt has transcended the form that his original vision of this music at first required, and thus were born the three "Sonetti del Petrarca" in the form they are most often heard today.

Liszt's investment in the expressive power of poetry and literature to inspire musical counterparts cannot be underestimated, no matter how subjective the relationship between them. Given the influence each of these sonnets had on Liszt's musical vision as he codified their sentiments in tone, I've included them here.

"Sonetto 47 del Petrarca" (Petrarch's Sonnet 47)

Blest be the year, the month, the hour, the day,
The season and the time, the point of space,
And blest the beauteous country and the place
Where first of two bright eyes I felt the sway
Blest the sweet pain of which I was the prey,
When newly doomed Love's sovereign law to embrace,
And blest the bow and shaft to which I trace
The wound that to my inmost breast found way:
Blest be the ceaseless accents of my tongue,
Unwearied breathing my loved lady's name:
Blest my fond wishes, sighs, and tears, and pains:
Blest be the lays in which her praise I sung,
That on all sides acquitted to her fair fame;
And blest my thoughts! For o'er them all she reigns.

In this poem, Sonnet 47, Petrarch pays homage to Laura, as well as the privilege of having met her. It is an impassioned paean, not so much to the spirit of a loved one as to his longing for her.

From the music's outset, Liszt finds just the right means of conveying in tone Petrarch's flight of passion. Here, Liszt captures Petrarch's description of Laura's enchanting gaze and the eyes that melted him. Swelling in the halo of a crescendo, an anxious sequence of chords, arguing for the supremacy of A major, rises chromatically from the tenor register in restless syncopations. In advance of the principal subject's entrance, Liszt gives voice to a fragmentary motivic plea in the form of a brief but chromatically inflected melodic strand, isolated by the right hand and confined to the alto register. This gentle quasi-soliloquy, though comprising only six notes over two bars, is set against arpeggiated chordal punctuations in the left and defined at its end by an expressive leap of a perfect fourth. Liszt then draws the figure out through repetition, elaborating and lengthening its motivic contours.

The principal subject that follows is cast in D-flat major. Anticipating it is a two-bar introduction in 6/4 time that exfoliates into a gently syncopated lullaby. Given its disjunct motion, this undulating theme is remarkably calm, though that is in part due to the rolling, rhythmically stable arpeggiations that support it in the left hand. The consequent of this theme likewise relies on syncopes to make its point, expanding its tenuous mood to include a halting procession of panting octaves that move steadily across a terrain of rapidly shifting harmonies.

The principal subject returns, its heart aflutter yet again but even more so, as Liszt has transposed it to G major and set it in a higher treble register. That G major stands at the distance of a tritone, a musical interval that spans three whole tones, from D-flat major is perhaps no accident; once again, the imposition of this heady if disconcerting tonal sea change is significant and psychologically affecting; the implicitly ambiguous character of a tritone, even when embodied by the juxtaposition of keys (as opposed to its manifestation within a single chord or interval), raises musical tension as it attenuates stability.

Once again, the music swells with octaves and a swift harmonic rhythm—that is, the rate at which harmony changes—that pushes the thematic material chromatically northward. In the space of only nine bars, Liszt flirts with E minor, C minor, A-flat major, F major, and D major. A quizzical dialogue ensues between an abbreviated variant of the ascending soliloquy that connected the introductory bars to the principal subject, and a quiescent halo of chords that glimmer in the upper reaches of the piano's treble register. As the key migrates yet again, to E major, a diaphanous stream of ornamental diminished chords leads back to a restatement of the principal subject.

Without warning, or even so much as dominant preparation, the key changes yet again as an ardent new theme surfaces and is given voice by the left hand in the tenor register. As D-flat major is the enharmonic equivalent to of C-sharp major—thus perching at the distance of a sixth above the previous key, E major, or a minor third below—the defining key relationship in this instance is governed by the submediant. Were it not for the expressive, sequential pulsations of double sixths that harmonize and accompany it in the right hand, this melody would seem wholly uneventful. After all, it is defined by only a single pitch that is repeated for four bars, save for its escape to a neighboring pitch a whole tone north in every other bar. The two-bar consequent hastens the pace as it articulates larger intervals, a major third and a perfect fifth. Liszt again raises the emotional stakes by elevating the theme, and its accompaniment in sixths, an octave higher.

A shrewd but sudden shift from D-flat major to A major points takes us back to the harmony of the introduction. A five-beat-long silence demarcates this passage from the ensuing coda, where a truncated recall of the introduction's consequent soliloquy emerges in D-flat major. An ornamental arpeggiation, standing alone and emulating bel canto, emerges from the cadence and ambles downward en route to a final restatement of the principal subject. This in turn drifts into a long silence—five beats modified by a fermata—en route to the close. The meter slows to four beats per bar as four chords, a mixture of dominant and secondary dominants, draw the work to its hushed and reverent end.

"Sonetto 104 del Petrarca" (Petrarch's Sonnet 104)

> Warfare I cannot wage, yet know not peace.
> I fear, I hope, I burn, I freeze again;
> Mount to the skies, then bow to earth my face;
> Grasp the whole world, yet nothing can obtain.
> His prisoner Love nor frees, nor will detain;
> In toils he holds me not, nor will release;
> He slays me not, nor yet will he unchain;
> No joy allows, nor lets my sorrow cease.
> Sightless, I see my fair, though mute, I mourn;
> I scorn existence, and yet court its stay;
> Detest myself, and for another burn;
> Bu grief I'm nurtured; and, though tearful, gay;
> Death I despise, and life alike I hate:
> Such, lady, dost thou make my wayward state!

Of all the Petrarch sonnets, this is the best known and certainly the most often played. Liszt published at least two versions for voice and piano, in 1846 and 1861, respectively, the first for tenor and the latter for baritone. Moreover, it is likely that its first incarnation, in 1838 or 1839, was also set for voice. Unfortunately, no manuscript exists, or if it does, it has not yet been discovered. There are two piano versions, the first of which is an elaborate and extraordinarily adventurous piece published in 1846, and the second and considerably more austere version found fame in the *Années de pèlerinage* as we know it today.

The work begins with a jagged, syncopated introduction that ascends chromatically in enriched octaves and, in the left hand, tenths. Though the four sharps in the key signature indicate that the prevailing tonality is E major, Liszt confounds our expectations as the work commences on the shoulders of a rootless V9 chord, thus imparting particular importance to the F-sharp in the treble. Adding to the harmonic ambiguity is a dominant seventh chord in the remote key of A-flat major that unfolds within the first four bars; just in case anyone might not notice, Liszt accents each of its constituents as it emerges. Though he spells the chord in flats, its relation to E major is not quite as remote as it first appears; A-flat, after all, is the enharmonic equivalent of G-sharp major and thus stands ion the relation of a mediant. The effect of this implicit bitonality is unsettling and destabilizing; together with the urgent, palpitating thrust of the syncopes en route to some as-yet-unknown destination, the sheer angst of it all becomes, in the space of only a few moments, discernable.

This four-bar introduction is not only dramatic, but a rhetorical necessity, as it bespeaks the concomitant anxieties and consternation of the poem itself. Indeed, Liszt duplicates in compositional terms the internecine conflicts and contrasting images that Petrarch establishes throughout his sonnet. The mood thus set is breathless, uneasy, and even belligerent for its determination to exhaust its potential, either in the form of even greater bluster or in relaxed resignation. "Pace non trovo!" (Peace I cannot find) is the impassioned outcry that opens Petrarch's poem and likewise finds its way, in Liszt's song, onto the pitch material in the fifth bar. For the piano transcription, the pianist would be well advised to keep those words in mind, as their combined trochaic and iambic rhythms contribute substantially to both the sense and motivic articulation of its musical counterpart. It is no accident that Liszt, precisely at this spot, changes the tempo to adagio and cadences on the dominant. (In the published song, the words drift into a recitative above the piano's pungent harmonic punctuations.)

After a brief rest, an ornamental flourish turns on the dominant and mediant simultaneously as it segues, by means of a descending arpeggio on a diminished chord and a tenuous stepwise ascent, to the principal theme in the alto register. This simple yet ardent tune, richly harmonized by arpeggiated chords below, proceeds in its first two bars with four repeated notes before it continues southward in stepwise motion to a half cadence. But as this four-bar phrase unfolds, it sports an expressive, syncopated leap of an octave, from E-natural to E-natural, before continuing its journey, in disjunct and stepwise chromatics, en route to its restatement.

Here the left hand takes over the melody, elaborating and ornamenting it an octave lower in the piano's tenor region. But its transformation is hardly complete; some six bars later, the right hand reiterates the principal subject verbatim in the treble, atop an oceanic pendulum of supportive arpeggios in the left. Thus far, this musical sonnet has proved itself the most operatic of the three.

A brilliant roulade accelerates to the upper registers of the piano in anticipation of a majestic restatement of the principal theme in expansive octaves in the upper reaches of the keyboard. In the left hand, a rich progression of rising and falling sixths lends new authority to this theme, which Liszt elaborates as an expansive, forceful, and voluminous arpeggio. A half cadence in G segues into a stream of descending double thirds, a penetrating double-note trill, and yet another restatement of the principal subject, now defined by thickly padded chords and octaves in the soprano and alto registers. The dynamic tension diminishes with the onset of an ever-so-delicate spray of rapidly descending sixteenths—thirty-three in all, over four beats—carved in diminution from a fragment of the second half of the principal subject.

Following a cadence in G major, the lyrical consequent of the principal subject is again made the melodic centerpiece. But here the texture has thinned to only two voices, as the left hand articulates a sequence of ascending arpeggios and the right gives voice to the theme. The mood is contemplative, melancholy, and resigned, as if to convey only a memory of the glories that had been, suggesting the pivotal ninth line of Petrarch's verse: "Sightless I see my fair; though mute, I mourn."

Another variant of the principal subject follows without fanfare and is rendered all the more turbulent, though quiescent, by the uneasy pulsations of sixteenths in the alto and tenor registers beneath it. Elsewhere, the bass slithers downward chromatically in an intermittent pattern of three-note sighs. Codifying the poet's despair in an improvisatory expanse of expressive octaves and a configuration of descending fourths and thirds, Liszt annihilates bar lines altogether en route to the eloquent coda.

In contradiction to the metrical irregularities of the introduction, which relied on syncopes to express anxiety, the coda moves forward heroically and straightforwardly in 4/4 time. It argues a variant of the introduction's consequent, which, as you recall, accompanied the words "Pace non trovo" in the published song. Here, the tempo slows a bit to "un poco più lento" as middle-range octaves, swelling with a mixture of pride and regret, take command of the melody. In support, the left hand intermittently punctuates the texture on the offbeats with widely spread chordal arpeggiations. This in turn segues into a final vision of grief, as for one last time, a fragment of the principal subject angles upward, in hushed chords, as if in a poignant reminiscence of a love never fully realized. A leap upward to the piano's registrational stratosphere plants a major third and thus establishes the dominant once again. A melting rivulet of thirds emanates and descends from this single exquisite moment as the left hand climbs upward through an unsettling arpeggio culled from the Neapolitan. The final four bars drift away in a sad prolongation of quarter-note and whole-note chords, its heartbreak made all the more painful by the inclusion of C-natural, the lowered sixth degree of the scale. A fermata extends the final tonic chord, which fades into the musical distance and vanishes, never to be heard from again—rather like Laura herself.

"Sonetto 123 del Petrarca" (Petrarch's Sonnet 123)

Yes, I behold on earth angelic grace,
And charms divine which mortals rarely see,
Such as both glad and pain the memory;
Vain, light, unreal is all else I trace;
Tears I saw shower'd from those fine eyes apace
Of which the sun ofttimes might envious be;
Accents I heard sighed forth so movingly,
As to stay floods, or mountains to displace,
Love and good sense, firmness, with pity join'd
And wailful grief, a sweeter concert made
Than ever yet was poured on human ear:
And heaven unto the music so inclined,
That not a leaf was seen to stir the shade,
Such melody had fraught the winds, the atmosphere.

The yearning romantic spirit that informs this ethereal confection and codifies Plutarch's ideal woman may seem light-years away from anything Beethoven ever composed. And yet a fundamental idea unites it to an aesthetic principle that Beethoven and the majority of his contemporaries broadly embraced. And that idea is the notion of the *sublime*.

The opposing forces, which the sublime was charged to reconcile in art, are likewise present in these Laura sonnets of Petrarch and thus are embodied abstractly in the object of his desire. As an emblem of passion and restraint, immeasurable love, and unattainable desire, "such as both glad and pain the memory" (to cite Petrarch himself in his Sonnet 123), she is, like all things sublime, the sum of her opposites.

Indeed, in this poem, Laura, like Dante's beneficent Beatrice, attains to transcendence. If in Petrarch's eyes she is just this side of divinity, it's with good reason: her presence, though disembodied, at once comforts, inspires, and enlightens him. For Liszt, the occasion is not so much one of paying tribute to Laura, or even to Petrarch's considerable poetic gifts, but to the aesthetic ideas that informed them.

As if to capture Petrarch's vision of "angelic grace" where "melody had fraught the winds, the atmosphere," Liszt inaugurates this tone poem in A-flat major with exceptional serenity. The slow tempo, lento placido, favors the likewise slow harmonic rhythm with which the work unfolds. A hush of oscillating sixths, configured as triplets and played by the right hand, hovers effortlessly astride a nearly static melodic fragment. Despite its melodic profile, this fragment—which is nothing more than a single note, F, twice repeated in the first bar and issued yet again in the second before falling by a fifth to B-flat—attains to a bona fide theme. Enshrouded by the hypnotic shimmer of the quiescent double sixths, the mood it sets is as transparent as it is ethereal. Or as Liszt was fond of saying to his students, "Es schwebt!" (It floats!).

The theme flourishes in a delicate expanse of open octaves in the upper register while the pulsating sixths in triplets continue to exfoliate below. Emerging from silence, a chromatic ascent in thirds edges upward from the alto register, and a variant of this figure does the same an octave higher, in a single voice, only moments later. The syncopated breaths that support it in the lower voices prepare the entrance of the lyrical principal subject that follows.

And here begins the song proper, so to speak. The first two bars of the melody here, tinged with regret, are a lithe, elegant affair that surveys every pitch in the A-flat scale, albeit not in scale order. Commencing on the dominant E-flat, the figure spirals upward by a major sixth to a C-natural, and from there to another E-flat an octave higher, before returning, in a gentle subdominant wash of stepwise and disjunct motion, to where it began. A two-bar consequent fills out the phrase period with an expressive ascent, through five eighth-notes, to F-natural, the sixth degree of the scale. The texture thickens as a patch of octaves, restrained but impassioned, give voice to a pleading dotted-note figure accompanied yet again by the pulsation of sixths in the left hand.

Here Liszt transforms the principal subject, altering its metrical organization as he widens the registration with octave doublings in the bass. Tension begins to mount en route to a climax as Liszt combines a fragment of the work's opening motive with the ascending five-note figure of the principal subject's consequent. But moments later, this same five-note figure assumes new proportions, availing itself of double sixths as the melody, now engorged on a chromatic ascension of octaves, reaches north to its *fortissimo* denouement in the remote key of E major.

An unexpected cadence on a stream of repeated E-naturals moves shrewdly toward a diaphanous restatement, in C major, of the principal subject, which Liszt has now rarefied and shrewdly positioned, within a triple *piano*, in an exceptionally high register of the instrument. To ensure the prevailing hush, he indicates una corda—that is, the use of the piano's left pedal, which shifts the dampers over to a single string on each note and thus reduces the instrument's volume capacity substantially. This is followed by an elegiac turn in the tenor voice, given over to the left hand, which, though preserving the overall quiescence, sings out a variant of the principal subject.

Here the anxious dotted figure, accompanied and harmonized by a diminished arpeggiation and a pedal point on E-flat below, returns and augurs another, more powerful climax. The double sixths take over the treble but have been reduced to a succession of anxious, sighing duplets (actually, as part of a triplet rhythm absent the first of its eighth-note constituents). These articulate the prevailing anxiety as the left does the same, but they do so out of phase and in quarter-note duplets. The musical temperature rises under a stringendo and a crescendo, culminating in a *fortissimo* climax astride a descending patch of dominant and secondary dominant chords.

The luxuriously ornamented return of the principal subject shifts to a diaphanous flutter of brilliant though quietly dispatched roulades. The introduction likewise resurfaces and migrates directly to the principal subject's second (five-note) consequent; evidently, Liszt felt that to push the first half of the principal subject yet again would have been to engage in thematic overkill. The music drifts upward and then downward in a reflective ascent of eighth-notes, before a gentle sequence of arpeggiations slows the tempo and brings the work to its languid conclusion.

"Après une lecture de Dante: Fantasia quasi sonata" (After Reading Dante: Fantasia Quasi Sonata, or "Dante" Sonata) (CD Track 2)

In this magniloquent work we encounter the augmented fourth (also known as a *tritone*), or *diabolus in musica*. Here it attains to something far grander than a harmonic coloration and becomes a compositional strategy in its own right. Indeed, in this work Liszt ingeniously exploits the implicit ambiguity of this special interval, and he does so wholly in the service of the poetic image the "Dante" Sonata seeks to paint.

Liszt penned his first version of the "Dante" Sonata (as the work has long been dubbed by pianists in lieu of its considerably longer title) in Italy in September 1839 and gave its premiere in November of that year; its working title at that time was "Fragment dantesque." It had been an interesting autumn, not only for Liszt and his erstwhile companion Marie d'Agoult, but for the rest of Europe. England was ready to do battle with China over opium, which the latter wanted destroyed and the former interpreted as interference in their customary business practices. In faraway America, the publication of Edgar Allan Poe's macabre poem *The Haunted Palace* stirred readers with its tale of evil and disembodied enchantments. And in Switzerland, a German chemist had discovered ozone. Liszt revised this piece ten years later, replacing its original title, "Fragment after Dante" with the much longer title "Prolégomènes à la Divina Commedia: Fantasie symphonique pour piano" (Preliminary Discourses on the Divine Comedy: A Symphonic Fantasy for Piano). Not until 1853 did he settle on the title with which we are familiar today.

Oddly enough, Liszt, whose principal language was French (not German or Hungarian, as myth would have it), somehow failed to correctly cite the title of Victor Hugo's poem, to which the work alludes. Indeed, the title of Hugo's poem, which Liszt culled from the latter's 1837 collection of fifty-one poems, is *Les voix intérieures* (Inner Voices). But it was Beethoven, not Hugo or Dante, who inspired the work's subtitle, "Fantasia quasi sonata." Liszt turned this moniker, which Beethoven attached to his two sonatas, Op. 27 (the first of which is the celebrated "Moonlight" Sonata), on its head, thus killing two birds of homage with one nominal stone.

Certainly, Hugo's poem informed Liszt's aesthetic disposition toward the musical realization that would become its eponym. But ultimately, the poem was less an inspiration for the music than it was a point of reference for its aesthetic purpose. Indeed, in *Les voix intérieures*, Hugo's poems are critiques of a number of celebrated artists and painters, of whom Dante was just one. Thus it was never Liszt's explicit intention to codify in any definitive way, programmatic or otherwise, Hugo's verse, but rather to show camaraderie of intent with the poet himself. Thus, like Hugo, Liszt hoped to convey, through his composition's exceptionally literary title, his own wholly unique interpretation of Dante Alighieri's (1265–1321) classic, the *Divine Comedy*.

And make no mistake: it was in fact Dante's poem, as much as Hugo's poetic reflections on it, that inspired Liszt. This 14,000-word epic is nothing if not a tale of woe, chronicling Dante's journey through the realm of the dead astride the wizened if ominous vision of the poet Virgil. The poem is fundamentally an allegory of Christian theology and is given over to the philosophical reflections of a man in the embrace of temptation (represented in the poem by beasts) and in search of personal redemption (symbolized by natural phenomena, such as mountains and the sun). Hell is not the only realm of the dead; heaven is, too, and Dante's tour of that upper region is led by Beatrice, herself a symbol of the ideal woman, or as artist of the romantic era would later envision, the eternal feminine. The principal constituents of this restless drama are the opportunists and outcasts, or shadows, which are the souls of the damned.

The opening of the work, which pays homage to sonata form without exactly conforming to it, begins with an evocation of hell. These are represented by an imperious trumpet-like fanfare, spelled out in a sequential descent of tritones in double octaves. Though the key signature is that of D minor, the tonality is ambiguous, especially owing to the imposition of the tritones, which cadence on an A-flat major triad; nothing could be more remote or alienated than that, though A-flat stands at the distance of a tritone from the tonic D. This impressive introduction continues for some twenty-nine measures en route to the exposition.

The inscription on Dante's gates of hell—"Abandon all hope, ye who enter here" (Lasciate ogne speranza, voi ch'intrate)—would appear to be a plausible interpretation of the introduction's opening motive, despite the protestation of August Stradahl, a student of Liszt who insisted it represented instead a plea to the spirits of the damned to step out of the shadows. That Liszt has arranged the initial motivic material in three sequential six-bar phrase periods—thus suggesting yet another diabolical symbol, 666—may be coincidence, but then again, given his Catholicism, perhaps not.

Beginning with the third sequence of tritones, which bellow forth in the piano's treble registers, Liszt invests in the power of silence, setting the tritones in a frame, as it were, of intermittent dramatic pauses. A crescendo accompanies a thickening of the texture into *fortissimo*, tritone-infested chords. Another pregnant pause is followed by a murky, ascending, and then descending passage in stepwise motion that is distinguished by the curious juxtaposition of the hands; here, the right mimics the left but does so out of phase, trailing its comrade on the weak beats at the metrical distance of a sixteenth.

A transitional passage ensues and takes all of six bars to forecast the repetitive motivic dimensions of the first subject—the murky beginnings of an exposition, if you will—that follows. Liszt accelerates the tempo, taking it from the opening "andante" to a stirring "presto agitato assai." The mood is grim as the shadows indeed step out, giving shape to a chromatically inflected sequence of duplet pulsations in octaves atop a tonic pedal point and a continual downward shift of diminished chords in the left hand. Though in general this is hardly program music, Liszt comes awfully close to it in this passage. Indeed, the dense chromaticism and offbeat thrusts that pit the right and left hand against each other in mimesis evokes the moans and wails of Dante's tortured spirits, as codified in the third canto of the *Inferno*:

> Here sighs, with lamentations and loud moans,
> Resounded through the air pierced by no star,
> That e'en I wept at entering. Strange tongues,
> Horrible cries, words of pain,
> Tones of anger, voices deep and hoarse,
> With hands together smote that swelled the sounds.
> Made up a tumult, that for ever whirls
> Round through that air with solid darkness stained,
> Like to the sand that in the whirlwind flies.

It was a student of Liszt, Walter Bache, who had inscribed this canto, along with annotations, in his personal copy of the score. From this

Walker intuits that it is not unreasonable to presume that Bache might have gleaned something from Liszt himself of this specific link of the music to its literary source. Whatever the case, and in the absence of a critical homology capable of linking the "Dante" Sonata's compositional data to the poem's verse—be that in rhythmic or organizational categories—there is neither risk nor shame in proffering, as Walker and others do, a definitive link between the two genres. Subjective though such an interpretation may be, Liszt certainly did not endow the work with its name for no reason.

What's more, Liszt instructs pianists to engage the damper pedal for a full five bars—the length of the entire phrase period. When carefully adjudicated by its performer, the resultant blur, modified further under the umbrella of a suave legato, sends a chill up the spine and seems deliberately render indistinct the ghostly apparitions. Making things all the more prescient is the dynamic, which is *piano*, but with persistent crescendo swells.

The grievous caterwauling, repeated a third time an octave higher, assumes an even more menacing shape as Liszt fattens the sonority by transforming the octaves, as well as the left-hand figure, into full-fledged chords. As this unrelenting jeremiad persists, it morphs into a painful dialogue between the soprano and alto registers in the right hand, before falling again, in a descent of distended octave tritones, onto a thorny transitional passage. Here a patch of octaves, followed by no-less-aggressive arpeggios, angles upward with terrifying ferocity. A chromatic descent of interlocking octaves debouches onto a pronouncement of the tritone motive, now made all the more resilient by the "più animato" that modifies its tempo and, more significantly, by a vigorous iambic rhythm.

With the onset of this phase of the transition, the tempo accelerates as the periodic delineation of a diminished seventh chord, outlined in a sequence of octave triplets, flourishes above. This brings to mind Charles Rosen's amusing observation that the profuse use of diminished chords numbers among Liszt's compositional weaknesses; in assigning this well-known chord structure a preeminent descriptive role as a means to convey fright, horror, or surprise, Liszt shamelessly engaged in cliché. And though that cliché may have been of the most delicious kind, Rosen refers to Liszt's particular fetish for diminished chords as both "over simple" and "insistent exploitation." Indeed, Rosen goes further to say that Liszt "shared this vice with contemporary composers of opera, who found the diminished seventh incomparably useful for effects of horror, rage, astonishment, and terror."

To his credit, at least, Liszt commingles tonalities as he climbs the chromatic ladder, jumping from G major to E-flat major to D-flat major in the blink of an eye, thus defeating any monotony that the diminished seventh sonorities, in the hands of a less skilled composer, might have caused.

Suddenly, the key changes to a bright F-sharp major, a tonality dear to Liszt's heart (as it was for Scriabin, on whom this work certainly exerted considerable influence a half century later) and one that he often used to convey heroic fortitude or spiritual greatness (not insignificantly, the "Benediction of God in Solitude" from *Harmonies poétiques et religieuses* and "Les jeux d'eaux à la Villa d'Este" from the third book of the *Années*—both of which we'll take a look at here—are likewise in F-sharp major). A torrent of powerful double octaves forms this second subject. Forceful and virulent, it alights alternately on thick tonic and dominant chords as it sweeps southward in triple *forte*, surveying the compositional landscape with the authority of a Valhallian god. These segue into the subject's consequent, a massive and impassioned reach of B-flat major triads that move upward in the right hand astride a tense pulsation of triplets in the left. A cadence on the dominant preceded a return to the introductory tritones and the full complement of its motivic consequents.

Oddly, this passage, which Walter Bache interpreted as a vision of Lucifer—a character that Dante barely refers to in the Divine Comedy—has more often than not been marginalized and dismissed as merely transitional. Transitional it is, but given its self-importance and thematic pretensions, it is also the work's second subject, as it broadly outlines a theme of its own. Indeed, the huge chords, which Liszt places squarely on the downbeats of each bar, though linked by the rush of descending octaves, form a majestic chorale. Motivically, the design of this chorale—that is, the relationship of the pitch material that forms its proliferation on the downbeats—is virtually identical to that of the first subject. Liszt expands the harmonic rhythm of the wailing, stretching it out, through the imposition and relationship of the chords, to essentially one pulsation per bar.

A word is in order here about the aesthetic agenda of pianists who, when faced with such blustery, virtuosic passagework, are obliged to make important artistic decisions. For a pianist, nowhere is the adjudication of artistic necessity in combination with technical agility more crucial. Liszt offers a great many temptations, which, if exploited for the wrong reasons—that is, for mere effect, rather than affect, and in an effort to please a crowd—can severely compromise the thrust and meaning of his music and harm the listener's experience of it. This is germane both to the interpretation and the manner in which we listen so much of Liszt's piano music. Indeed, in order to make musical sense of it all, something more is needed. Pianists whose principal objective is to extol mechanical over aesthetic values can easily impress a listener with the speed and fury of their octaves. Certainly, virtuoso pianists should easily be able to fly through any concentrated flurry of prestissimo octaves, double notes, and glittering arpeggios. But what distinguishes the merely facile from the artistic is the ability to articulate these pianistic constituents with affective finesse and musical forethought.

Though it is true that the thrilling, purely acrobatic dimensions of Liszt's piano works form an integral part of their sound world as well as their aesthetic purpose, they cannot thrive on empty display. Authentic virtuosity embraces so much more—rhythmic, harmonic, and structural cognizance; affective inflection; and polyphonic transparency, for example. In the case of the aforementioned passage, the proliferation of fiery octaves provides only a means to an end; the octaves are links in a very grand chain indeed, filling in the space that separates the blustery tonic and dominant chords that ring out, on the downbeat of each bar, from the upper and lower registers of the instrument.

Thus it is the pianist's job to make sure that the connection between these chords—the intonational glue, so to speak—is made clear, so that we, as listeners, are made aware that each of these massive chords bleeds over time into another. As for the octaves, even these ought project a melodic attitude, their rhythmic and affective trajectory assured by their harmonic orientation and purpose, as opposed to merely being thrown off like so much artillery fire. On the accompanying CD, you can hear Claudio Arrau, a pianist of uncommon musical authority, shape the passage into a lyrical profusion, thus refusing to make of the litany of octaves something merely busy, vapid, and aggressive.

But now let's return to the work at hand. On the heels of the heroic octave chorale, the wailing shadows are likewise revisited. But now the mood is neither anguished or painful but is quiet, resigned, and contemplative. Here, the dramatic contrast with the previous passage waxes extreme as the triple *forte* diminishes suddenly to triple *piano*. The chorale emerges yet again in the piano's middle register but is now transformed into a quiescent, even submissive variant of its first incarnation. A stream of triplets undulates beneath its now familiar theme.

Alfred Brendel (but not Liszt) refers to this theme, marked "Andante," as the Francesca da Rimini episode. Francesca da Rimini, a contemporary of Dante alluded to in the *Commedia*'s second circle of hell, was an unwitting, though not unwilling, adulteress. Deceived into marrying the brother of the man she was engaged to—and whom she had never laid eyes on—Francesca was the ultimate victim. Though she was murdered by her husband, the ideology of medieval Catholicism, renounced her as a harlot. Thus her punishment is a consequence of the lust that devoured her. As Brendel reminds us, citing Dante's canto, "There is no greater sorrow than to remember happy times while in misery."

As the arpeggiated consequent of the chorale—in the first instance, the procession of ascending B-flat major triads, but now articulating a D major chord—angles upward in the baritone register, its mournful soliloquy awash in regret, the right hand plays a sequence of weepy, descending sixths. The texture thins to a single melodic line in imitation of a recitative as the tempo slows to an adagio and comes to a half cadence.

The vision of the sublime that follows ushers in the development and takes us from the gates of hell to the portals of heaven. Indeed, here Liszt affords us a glimpse of Dante's *Paradiso*. The composer now engages polyrhythms; six sixteenths in the right hand against four in the left hover over a dominant pedal point in the bass and, by proxy, in the tenor voice, as well, where C-sharp is permanently embedded in the likewise arpeggiated tonic triad. As we shall see, this sultry, circular, if somewhat ambiguous rhythm is most likely meant to convey an image of the divine. What's more, Liszt specifically double stems the uppermost notes—the melodic partials, if you will—in the right hand, configuring them as offbeat duplets. For its part, the right hand covers a rather wide keyboard terrain, circling around the alto and soprano registers in a continuous arpeggiation, as the left hand unfolds below in descent.

In the context of the triple *piano* that modifies it, the complex and unsettling polyrhythms, and Liszt's unusual direction to play in an improvisatory manner ("Più tosto ritenuto e rubato quasi improvisato"), the effect is remarkable. Together with the hypnotic, continual rotation of arpeggios, the high tessitura of the outer pitch material in the right hand evokes the twinkling pulsations of starlight in a night sky. This is brought home all the more by the discreet emphasis of these pitches—arranged as offbeat duplets—that the double stems require. While it may not cause anyone to experience, in some miraculous revelation, a vision of Christ and the Virgin Mary, as Dante did on his journey to paradise, it comes close enough to musical magic. A more enchanting moment in this or any other work of Liszt would be hard to find.

This figure is an ideal example of contrapuntal melody, wherein what appears to be a single melodic line actually comprises two or more themes, albeit out of phase with each other and its constituents connected one to the other not in succession, but across space and time. Thus, in this instance, the A-sharps in the alto voice might be construed as belonging to each other as they move on, in the second bar of the section, to B-natural. Likewise, the F-sharps above form to a line of their own in juxtaposition to the E-sharps that follow in the ensuing bar. And atop all this are the double-stemmed pitches, which taken together constitute yet another melodic presence. Elsewhere in the lowest register, yet another figure—a chromatic accompaniment—ascends stealthily in support.

The net effect brings us back to an image in the Divine Comedy, wherein Beatrice guides Dante through the nine celestial spheres of heaven. The atmosphere is entirely transparent, the mood at once ethereal, crepuscular, and glimmering. Like the heaven of Dante's invention, where paradise is at once cylindrical and concentric, the rotation of notes in this heady figure bears witness to a rarefied vision, perhaps akin to the sphere of fixed stars and the Primum Mobile that Dante describes so elegantly in cantos 25–29. Here, there is no need for the corporeal; in this enlightened sphere, existence, such as we know it, has become pure concept. The constellations themselves are but an expression of God and love.

Liszt raises the stakes as the figure ascends higher and higher and becomes increasingly impassioned. Metrical accents shift into a more conventional triplet configuration in both hands; the consequent of the principal subject—the wailing of the shadows—surfaces again, now embedded as a single voice within the weak beats of the left hand. The pace accelerates gradually and culminates, on the heels of a crescendo, in an imperious, swooshing arpeggio.

A brusque three-measure sequence of descending scales in unison leads to a new passage. Here, the *diabolus in musica* is cast in an even pulsation of dissonant chords in the left hand, made all the more pungent by the inclusion of open fifths. Above, the right-hand toys with a descending flurry of tritone anapests. A menacing tremolando, punctuated by a mixture of hobbling staccato interjections and anapest tritones, paints a demonic picture indeed. These segue into the principal subject in more or less its original configuration; here the shadows, committed to misery, wail once again.

But now the shadows are cut short in what might be construed, were this ordinary sonata form, as the beginning of a development. Here, octaves rule the day. A wave of ascending octaves, in consecutive groups of six, presses forward under a brisk stringendo, that is, a cumulative acceleration of tempo. These debouche onto yet another spate of tritone anapests, which now mix vigorously with intermittent onslaughts of octaves in contrary motion, perfect fourths and fifths, and dissonant minor sevenths. A triple *forte* serves to welcome a particularly belligerent battery of rising octaves in the left hand alongside a blast of widespread major chords, two to a bar, in the right. No sooner do they begin than the left-hand octaves disintegrate into jumpy but sequentially organized pairs, each of which is separated by an eighth-rest. Astride it, the right hand holds on to its play of powerful chords, now sautéing boldly from alto to soprano register in a devilish jump.

You'd think that, at this point, Liszt would wind things down a bit and come to cadence. But he does not, choosing instead to intensify the activity with yet another sequential parade of octaves. After a while, so many octaves, in just as many contexts, tax the interpretive imagination of the pianist who takes on this work. But onward he goes, nevertheless. Now the right hand takes over as the tempo is again heightened and a barrage of octaves, outlining diminished chords, exfoliates. The tritone anapests, now taken over by the left hand, also embed themselves in diminished chords.

The octaves, drawn down to the bass atop blustery chordal figurations in the left hand, segue into a quiet recall of the chorale theme, now set up in the left-hand chords as the bass rumbles ominously, like distant thunder (or timpani!), below. The dynamic dwindles to *pianissimo* as echoes of the anapest ornament the bass. The music slows, sputters out, and drifts into three beats of abject silence before emerging again in a recall of the principal subject. Now Liszt is more explicit, instructing the pianist to play lamentoso (with lament) as the shadows resurface, but at a somewhat slower pace; the passage recasts the material in the far leaner texture of open octaves in the right hand and only light chordal punctuations in the left. The shadows, exhausted and resigned to their fate, have now become only a shadow, you might say, of their former selves.

After ten bars, the shadows have petered out altogether, leaving only silence and two intermittent octave bursts in *pianissimo*. What follows is the already familiar iambic motive, but now in an altered state; as if making an effort to renounce the authority of the tritone, it announces itself feebly, in triple *piano* and in the form of descending open fifths and perfect, not augmented, fourths. A fermata signals a long pause en route to the breaking of another kind of dawn, or another vision of heaven.

A clarion call of thirds and fifths in the alto register transforms the chorale theme into something otherworldly. Twittering above, a tremolando, giving voice to major triads without a tritone in sight, breezes by within the sustained hush of a *pianissimo*. If redemption is at hand here, it is not quite ready for the sinner of this drama. Moments later, another passage of weighty double octaves ascends in unison en route to the final statement of the chorale, which has swelled again to triple *forte*. But now the rapid volley of octaves that punctuated it earlier have morphed into quarter-note chords, which exploit nearly the full registrational range of the piano. Widely spaced chords, octaves, and arpeggios lead to the introduction's tritones, splayed out by the left hand in vivacious octaves astride a vibrant tremolando in the right.

A restless coda ensues, its mood enhanced by sequences of breathless chords played by the left hand in syncopation. Again Liszt brings the full range of the piano into play, orchestrating it as if were a *fortissimo* barrage of trumpets, trombones, strings, and woodwinds in tutti. As the tempo moves northward to presto, a biting, satirical variant of the shadows' wail imposes itself in enormous octave and chordal leaps in both hands. Here, Liszt plays with the devil himself, who mocks the proceedings as he hobble-foots his way to the conclusion. With the right hand played off the beat and out of phase with the left, it is a monstrously difficult thing for a pianist pull off effectively. Indeed, this is no mere mechanical exercise, but a challenge to the interpreter to invest the figure with meaning and to give it the lyrical shape it demands.

And how do first-rate pianists do that, exactly? Well, for starters, they must identify the central crux of each four-bar phrase period—that is, where in the phrase the greatest dynamic emphasis ought to be placed. Liszt was shrewd to demand the passage be played *piano*, thus making its execution that much trickier. If the figure is to emerge as both light-footed and transparent, the interpreter is obliged to inflect its thematic constituents, illuminating its affective character; if the notes are equalized and made to sound mechanical, it will fall flat and its shape will become unintelligible. A slight emphasis or, better yet, lengthening, on the first and third octaves, for example, in every bar would do the trick as a means to project a melodic attitude. Or, as Roberto Poli shrewdly intuits in his performance, a discreet emphasis of the right hand's leap of a fourth and a fifth (in the middle of the third and fourth bars, respectively) lends the passage a lyrical elegance that a less gifted artist might deny it.

However, there is also a school of thinking that prefers an even-handed, wholly mechanical approach that would render each constituent equal; the aesthetic point of view espoused by that mindset holds that whatever is mechanical is essentially inhuman and thus the metaphorical cum aesthetic equivalent of evil. There are those who prefer the former and those who prefer the latter approach. But if executed with authority and good judgment, and not merely as a matter of mindless physical caprice, each point of view is valid.

The devil's mockery draws to a close astride a chromatic ascent of major chords, still out of phase between the hands, which plummet into the shadows' subject. Now fully restored to its original configuration, this now all-too-familiar wail cries out yet again for some eight bars before abruptly arriving on a mass of chords, three to a bar, in D major. While maintaining a marchlike rhythm, this chordal procession modulates at a furious pace, alighting on a new harmony in each successive bar. Indeed, Liszt carries us forward from D major, to C major, then to B-flat major, A-flat major, and finally, F-sharp major, where things finally come to cadence.

A recall of the imperious iambic rhythm that has so often defined the tritone passages in this piece surfaces again as the tempo slows to andante. But here the diabolus in musica has been defeated and replaced by an open fifth. In the bass below, a bristling tremolando on a D major triad pulsates for four full bars, while a descent of D major chords, giving emphasis to the perfect fourths and open fifths that constitute them, make their way to the work's final chord. But that chord, though ostensibly D major, is missing its third, F-sharp, which would render its tonality definitive. Thus it embeds within itself a question mark, as if there were room for the devil to win. As the "Dante" Sonata comes to its glorious end, hell evidently has not yet frozen over.

"Venezia e Napoli" (Venice and Naples), S. 162

Liszt gave originally gave birth to his breezy, elegant "Venezia e Napoli," a kind of suite within a suite, in 1840. But in 1859 he revisited the work, revising it and then publishing it two years later in 1861 as a supplement to the second book of the *Années de pèlerinage*.

Three works make up “Venezia e Napoli”: “Gondoliera” (Gondolier’s Song), “Canzone,” and “Tarantella.” A gondolier song informs each of the first two: in “Gondoliera,” it is Giovanni Peruchini’s “La biondina in gondoletta,” and in the “Canzone,” it’s “Nessun maggior dolore” from Rossini’s opera *Otello* (which is yet another allusion to Dante; it refers to a famous phrase from the Divine Comedy’s *Paradisio*, mentioned earlier: “There is no greater sorrow than to remember happy times when one is pain”). For the devilishly impressive final work, “Tarantella,” Liszt appropriates themes of another composer, Guillaume-Louis Cottrau (1797–1847), who, despite his Gallic origins (he was born in France), was every bit as Italian in culture and sensibility as the Venetian gondolier Liszt’s music portrays.

“Gondoliera”

Opening this lyrical trio is the “Gondoliera,” a lilting barcarolle in A major that begins with an oscillating ostinato in the left hand that expands into a hushed ascent of arpeggiated sixteenths in the right. The quiescent introduction hemorrhages into the principal theme, a gentle, endearing F-sharp major. It is a fragrant, lyrical profusion in double thirds that slides gently forward astride yet another arpeggiated tonic-chord ostinato below.

Like Chopin’s *Berceuse*, this gentle work unfolds on the order of a developing variation, deftly elaborating its original eight-bar theme by enveloping it with ornaments and delicate sonic brocades. Liszt draws it subtly forward into a vortex of diaphanous trills, played by both the right and left hands in the soprano and alto registers while the theme, now cast in quiescent double thirds in a higher register, propels itself forward. As the left hand takes over the theme in thirds, the right expands *pianissimo* into a refined filigree of arpeggios, trills, and double notes. A resigned coda sees a thickening of the theme into chords, played by both hands as *pianissimo* drifts to the almost imperceptible dynamic of a double *pianissimo*.

For the pianist, the difficulty here is neither speed nor the navigation of the litany of arpeggios. Rather, the musical issues here demand a player capable of manipulating, the quiescent undulations with seamless aplomb. The music virtually hovers, and to sustain its sense of weightlessness is not easy. Any attempt to give undue weight on the downbeats, for example, will serve only to interrupt continuity and smother the transparency of the sonorities.

"Canzone"

Much the same can be said for "Canzone," the dolorous gondolier's song in E-flat minor, that Liszt sets in the middle of this trio of supplementary works. A strongly articulated double-dotted motive sings out boldly as it descends in stepwise progression in the alto register astride a rapid tremolando in the left hand. Only five bars into the work, this melody relocates to the bass register as the pianist crosses the right hand over the left. The mood is unusually serious, yet also lyrical and sensuous. As the melody expands into octaves, the registrational distance likewise expands; the tremolando parts ways with the theme with the magisterial assurance of Moses parting the Red Sea. A passionate outburst of octaves segues to an airy arpeggiated oscillation in the left hand as the principal dotted motive, now tamed by *pianissimo* and thrown handily to the piano's uppermost register. The final bars see the return of this now compelling tune to the bass, while the tremolando pulsates below and diminishes to *pianissimo.*

"Tarantella"

The crown of this musical triumvirate is the spirited "Tarantella" in G minor. This virtuoso vehicle opens with a vivid bass grumble pitting a rising bass progression against slurred duplets in the right hand played off the beat. The jaunty principal theme ensues some thirty-seven bars later, its eight-bar phrase period articulated by a vibratory thrust of repeated notes and harmonized by a single chord, played by the left hand, on the fourth beat of each bar.

A new thematic episode configured in rising chords and octave follows, only to be dovetailed by a swift decent of sixteenths in the high soprano register. As the tempo accelerates, Liszt introduces yet another theme, a rollicking procession that turns around on itself like a dog chasing its own tail. The return of the principal theme in repeated notes moves discreetly into a wispy, *pianissimo* codetta that cadences onto G minor chords.

Here, Liszt introduces an immensely appealing Neapolitan tune that recalls the sultry dotted rhythm of the 'Canzonetta," yet again enshrouding it in a four-bar phrase. The tune moves northward by half steps astride a rolling procession of broken chords and a pedal point in the lower voices. Liszt elaborates the theme, giving way to ornamental passagework in double sixths and just the sort of florid material normally reserved, in the vocal medium, for a coloratura soprano. A variant of the principal theme shines through a scintillating passage in rapid repeated notes, before morphing once again in the guise of arpeggiations gracefully divided in contrasting motion between the hands.

The tempo accelerates to sempre prestissimo as Liszt launches the work's thrilling coda. A torrent of colossal interlocking chords and octaves brings the work to a thrilling close in G major.

"Troisième année" (Third Year), S. 163

As we have seen, this final set of the *Années de pèlerinage*, which Liszt composed between 1867 and 1877, is a summation of his lifelong journey.

"Angelus! Prière aux anges gardiens" (Prayer to the Guardian Angels)

"Angelus! Prière aux anges gardiens" (Prayer to the Guardian Angels) is at once a study in quiescence and the codification of bell music in tone. The delicate wash of alternating octaves and perfect fourths that inaugurate it were, according to Liszt himself (or more accurately after the account of an English visitor, Hugh Reginald Haweis, whom he received at his rooms at the Villa d'Este), a musical portrait of Italian bell changes, or "angelus." The work's texture is astonishingly sparse, its largely diatonic, open-ended melodies adrift and irresolute throughout. The piece is set in the bright key of E major, and the tempo marking is simply Andante pietoso, which imparts more about the character of the piece as Liszt envisioned it than it does the pace. Echoes of Wagner's *Parsifal* surface here and there as the work's pious demeanor expands into a *fortissimo* chordal sequence. (Oddly, and though it is rarely if ever performed this way today, Liszt doubles the piano with another instrument, the harmonium, for eight bars in advance of the return of the opening bell theme.) The final thirty-three measures give shape to an exceptionally lean thematic fragment that shines, like an evening star, from the highest regions of the piano. The work draws to its serene, unharmonized close in *pianissimo*, its oddly modest melody having been entrusted to the right hand alone.

"Aux cyprès de la Villa d'Este I: Thrénodie" (To the Cypresses of the Villa d'Este I: Threnody)

With that, we come to the first of the two "threnodies" (laments), which were inspired not only by Liszt's melancholy at the time, but also by the great Villa d'Este, or more precisely, by the ancient cypresses that abut it. But as the natural and not-so-natural beauties of the Villa d'Este also inspired the fourth and most famous work in the set, "Les jeux d'eau à la Villa d'Este," it might be helpful to take a closer look at the Villa d'Este itself, as it provided Liszt with such a rich source of inspiration.

The Villa d'Este lies some thirty-four kilometers east of Rome in the Piazza Trento, which is in the Lazio region near Tivoli. To this day, this remarkable expression of Renaissance aesthetics remains one of the most popular tourist spots in Europe. Commissioned in 1550 by the region's governor, the Cardinal Ippolito II d'Este, it is the creation of the sixteenth-century mannerist architect Pirro Ligorio. A lavishly appointed estate, its compound includes buildings, elaborately terraced gardens, and, most notably, a network of more than five hundred fountains. Liszt kept a suite of rooms on the top floor of the villa in 1869, taking up residence there intermittently some four years after having entered, in Tivoli, the minor orders of the priesthood.

In the late summer of 1877, when Liszt returned to his quarters at the Villa d'Este, his mood was dark. He had been suffering from bouts of depression and nervous anxiety. Perhaps already gleaning that the end was near, this man of letters and international adulation put on a brave face for his students and the public but could not escape the melancholy that besieged him.

Inspired by the rows of stately ancient cypresses that ornament the grounds of the villa, Liszt felt somehow at one with these noble flora, as if their gravitas and antiquity was somehow on par with his own. Indeed, the solemnity of the first "Cyprès" in G minor reveals itself in a procession of repetitive octaves in the bass, a major third, pragmatically speaking, but which Liszt configures mysteriously as diminished fourths from B-flat to F-sharp. These form the introduction to the work, lending to it the ambience of a funeral pedal point. The somewhat turgid harmonies played by the right hand proceed upward chromatically, in octaves defined by the built-in perfect fourths and hollow open fifths; indeed, the atmosphere is positively medieval, even sepulchral.

Some thirty-three measures into the work, the principal theme emerges from the musical darkness. It is a variant, or extension, really, of the first theme, its four-bar chromatic configuration distinguished by the inclusion of a rising minor sixth in its middle. The gentle suspension that rumbles throughout the left hand below serves at once to destabilize the rhythmic tension as it buffets the phrase, in the context of a powerful crescendo, toward an anguished appassionato climax in *fortissimo* only a few bars later.

The mystery of the music's middle section is in part determined by a change of key; though Liszt eliminates the key signature here, suggesting a move into C major, the ambiguous tonality is a hybrid of D major and F-sharp minor. Here, the principal theme hovers in the tenor register above a quiet oscillating bass in eighth-notes. An extraordinarily lengthy crescendo complements an accelerando as the theme migrates northward in minor thirds. As it does, the key moves to F-sharp minor, while the right hand gives voice to an array of slow-moving arpeggios.

These culminate in an anguished passage of out-of-phase dissonances cast in thick chords that pile atop one another as if in search of resolution. Liszt again alters the key signature to a single sharp as the work evolves into E minor. An ominous tremolando growls ominously in triple *forte* in the bass while the principal theme mutates into fragments of its original. The dynamic dips to *pianissimo* as the left hand, without the accompaniment of the right, articulates a chromatic descent, again in tremolando, from C-sharp to B-natural. The heart-wrenching return to a dissonant recall of the climactic consequent of the principal theme, now unmistakably cast in rising octaves in the right hand with a slightly delayed arpeggiation of the left that anticipates the symbolic redemption that ensues. A chromatically inflected procession of chords drifts from *piano* to *fortissimo* and winds down chromatically with migratory prowess. The work draws to its sad but somewhat ethereal conclusion with an alternation of major and minor chords in remote tonalities—C minor and C major—before alighting, in the final bar, in G major.

"Aux cyprès de la Villa d'Este II: Thrénodie" (To the Cypresses of the Villa d'Este II: Threnody)

In the second of the "Cyprès" pieces, Liszt pays tribute to Wagner, or at least to the famous opening harmonic progression of act 3 of the latter's opera *Tristan und Isolde*. It is not so much a direct citation as a gesture of admiration for the aesthetic potential of Wagner's ingenious harmonic invention.

The mood here is one of bleak austerity, which is further amplified by the lean textures, immanently ambiguous augmented fourths (the aforementioned *diabolus in musica*), and persistent movement in unison octaves. The principal theme, configured in octaves in the piano tenor and bass registers, makes itself known some thirty bars into the work; it is an odd tune, if you can call it that, that avails itself of a rising perfect fifth and a likewise ascending perfect fourth before moving in stepwise motion to F, only to turn around again in the last measure of this four-bar phrase. Indeed, as the tempo accelerates in an emboldened march of octave doublings, marked "poco animato," Liszt sets his harmonic ship adrift in B-flat major and then, only a few bars later, sails into B-flat minor.

Lowering the musical temperature to a mere outline of chromatically inflected unisons in the bass, Liszt codifies his wanderlust in F-sharp major in a rising and falling series of major arpeggios. The evanescent cypresses sway ever so elegantly in an oddly resigned octave theme that descends in major seconds and minor thirds and brings the onset of the troubled inner chromaticism of the following section. Here, a chromatic pulsation in eighth-notes, given over to the alto and tenor voices against the soprano register's slower-moving ascent, offers a glimpse of things to come.

The principal theme, now cast in A-flat major and entrusted to the bass astride a mysterious tremolando in the right hand, segues to the bold octave refrain, in B-flat major, of the opening. As the key migrates to E major, it is again arrested by a quiet procession of ascending arpeggios for which, only fifteen bars later, Liszt abandons bar lines altogether, reducing it to a freewheeling chromatic fragment in the alto register. All but the last four of the concluding nineteen bars survey an arpeggiated descent of broken dominant, subdominant, and mediant chords that move southward from the lofty soprano register to the bass. The last four measures articulate a single line, in the alto, punctuated by an F-double-sharp—the raised second degree of the E major scale—thus conveying, one last time and with unmistakable prescience, the idea of the last breath.

"Les jeux d'eaux à la Villa d'Este" (The Fountains of the Villa d'Este) (CD Track 3)

Much has been written about the inspiration "Les jeux d'eaux à la Villa d'Este" held for Liszt's successors, not the least of whom were Debussy and Ravel. There is no end of discussion about how it so generously adumbrates the impressionist music (a misnomer, as Debussy's work had far more in common aesthetically with symbolism than with French impressionism) of Debussy and Ravel, and particularly the latter's own work of almost the same name, *Jeux d'eau.*

Composed in 1877, "Les jeux d'eaux à la Villa d'Este" at once reflects Liszt's spiritual pretensions and his compositional ambitions. As Alan Walker observes, Liszt virtually sanctified his works that treated religious themes or ideas by casting them in F-sharp major, a key he evidently associated with all things holy. In this regard, "Les jeux d'eaux à la Villa d'Este" bears much in common with "Bénédiction de Dieu dans la solitude" (Blessing of God in Solitude, from *Harmonies poétiques et religieuses*), with "St. François d'Assise: La prédication aux oiseaux" (Saint Francis of Assisi Preaching to the Birds, from *Deux légendes*), and also, in my view, with one of his more rarefied creations, the ethereal Impromptu in F Sharp.

"Les jeux d'eaux à la Villa d'Este" is considerably more than the sum of its parts. Wagner and his wife, Cosima, Liszt's daughter, were among the first to hear it in the spring of 1878, when Liszt played it for them privately at their residence at Wahnfried. Wagner was not terribly impressed, finding the work to be little more than descriptive program music. Certainly, the continually self-absorbed Wagner, whose musical priorities extended only so far as his own work, could not be bothered to dig deeper in the presence of mere piano music.

But from Liszt's perspective, this piece, though inspired by the Villa d'Este's magnificent fountains, remains on the order of a confessional; it was an expression of his Catholic fervor. An exercise in music-aquatic imagery it was not. Indeed, the allusion to water, which he codifies in the continuous streams of glittering arpeggios, trills, and tremolos that inform it, was symbolic. In fact, it was Liszt's response to a verse from the Gospel According to St. John (4:14): "Sed aqua quam ego dabo ei, fiet in eo fons aquae salientis in vitam aeternam" (But whosoever drinketh of the water that I shall give him, shall never thirst, but shall have everlasting life"). So that no one could make any mistake about that, Liszt cited the verse in the score, tacking it above the onset of the ethereal D major section about halfway through the work. With this, Liszt offered sanctuary, in the form of music that so serenely encapsulated them, not only for his religious aspirations, but for the idea, now become aesthetic principle, of eternity itself.

As the work proceeds in 2/4 time, mensural space is at a premium; not a moment is wasted. An ascending spray of thirty-second-note arpeggios, constructed around the dominant seventh, inaugurates the piece. As this glistening sequence rises from the piano's alto register to the upper reaches of the keyboard, it is grounded, for the first six bars, by a persistent pedal point on C-sharp. There is no melody per se, but only a fluid harmonic migration from dominant to tonic, with patches of subdominant and other dominant-quality chords, en route to the long-delayed principal subject. The harmonic rhythm thus far is slow; the harmony changes with each successive bar. But then the thirty-second-note patterns ascend again as the C-sharp pedal point, like a rocket booster falling back to earth, releases its hold. With the figure's upper notes articulating the first half of a G-sharp major scale, the pattern rises to high D-sharp as the harmonic rhythm increases. Now the harmony shifts with each successive arpeggio, or twice per bar, before descending again to the piano's middle registers. Here the configuration changes to a kind of fanciful shimmer of broken fifths, which alight on a no-less-vibratory tremolo in thirds.

Liszt relaxes the tension briefly, eliminating the flurry of thirty-second notes and replacing them with only two solid chords per bar. These in turn segue into the beginning of the principal subject, a diaphanous four-bar oscillation of thirds on the tonic, played ever so quietly by the right hand in the piano's high treble and set astride a hushed tremolo in the left hand. Adumbrating by some thirty years the nearly identical motive in Debussy's plush character piece for piano *L'isle joyeuse*, the left hand then proffers, as a consequent, an important new motive. Outlining a tonic triad, it is a mercurial sixteenth-note triplet followed immediately by two eighths and a whole-note modified by a vivacious trill. The figure repeats, before moving into a new motive, which can be interpreted either as the second subject or as a subtle variant of the first. With the right hand still a-flurry in tremolo, the left hand emerges here with a lyrical stepwise profusion in the tenor voice, configured in eighths and functioning as an ornament—it is a turn. With this material, Liszt expands the phrase period to six bars.

Suddenly the persistent tremolos, which have informed the work thus far, dissolve entirely. That Liszt has abandoned them with such shrewd dispatch is remarkable enough, but more significant still is the perceptible change of texture. Here, yet one more new motivic fragment, a third subject, rears its head in the left hand's alto, giving shape to a gentle theme that ascends and descends over nine bars in minor thirds and stepwise motion. Above it, the right hand, surveying a span of two octaves, has morphed from arpeggios to a procession of rising and falling double thirds.

The texture thins as the double thirds float away, leaving only a single strand before the reemergence of the principal subject, now fleshed out in somewhat fuller chords and with the addition of a voice in the tenor register. The tremolos also make their return here. Following a restatement of the second subject's mercurial sixteenth-note triplet, Liszt brings back the third the melodious third subject with its airy wash of double thirds in the right hand above. These Liszt expands and elaborates in descending four-bar sequences punctuated again by trills. Not finished yet, Liszt now shows his true colors and the immanent strategy of this work to be none other than our old friend, thematic transformation. As the right hand takes off anew in a parade of scintillating arpeggios, the left hand gives voice to a variant, in sixths, of the earlier third subject. Without fanfare, the right hand exchanges arpeggios for a stream of ascending double thirds, this time proceeding in stepwise motion and then in intervallic descent, as the left hand engages a two-bar-long trill below.

The tension heightens in the ensuing twenty-four bars, which are illuminated by the left hand's lyrical procession of sixths and a swoop of rising and falling arpeggios in the right. With the reemergence of the first subject in E major, now arpeggiated in thick chords in the left hand, Liszt codifies exaltation; the mood is ecstatic, even frenetic. Following a spirited patter of lightly inflected rotation of arpeggios that drifts southward atop a tremolo, the key changes to D major. Here the first subject, assuming celestial status, is thrown into relief, as it were, in the upper registers of the keyboard and set atop yet another wide rotation of arpeggiated chords in the left. This is the site of the aforementioned citation from the Gospel According to St. John. The tonality shifts, flirting with the remote keys of F major and E-flat major, before returning to the home key of F-sharp major. Here the rolling arpeggios in the left hand thrive as the right restores the lyrical second subject, with its ornamental, built-in turn, in octaves above. The lyrical third subject, embedded by the right hand in the upper register, follows and crescendos into an impassioned climax on the dominant as a trill shudders ecstatically in the left.

The key shifts again, to the subdominant A major. A rising sequence of octaves looms from the bass below, while the right hand grumbles ominously in a rolling pattern of alternating octaves, thirds, and fifths. Liszt engages a three-hand effect here, too, demanding double duty of the left hand, which spells out its material in octaves and doubles the fragment of the upper voice in imitation at the distance of a fourth. As these descend into a tremolo in the bass, a patch of octaves, proceeding in eighths, swells up in the right hand. The key shifts back to F-sharp major as the octave expanse is twice more repeated and ascends, *fortissimo*, to a high B-natural. Here a descent of unison octaves explodes the duple meter, giving emphasis to weak beats and attenuating the strong ones over the bar line.

A final, autumnal surge of rich arpeggios outlines a dominant ninth, entrusted to the left hand, and emerges lustily from the bass. Like a tolling bell, a D-sharp in an open octave repeats three times before the arpeggio rises swiftly and voluminously to the upper reaches of the soprano register. Liszt echoes the passage in sequence, rising in diminuendo in stepwise motion en route to the coda. Here he asks the pianist to slow down a bit and returns to the ornamental second subject, now relegated to a passage of octaves, astride that ever-present tremolo, in the soprano register. As the tremolo elevates itself to the right hand, the left brings back the principal subject, now arpeggiated in thick chords, in E-flat major. Perhaps to avoid any harmonic pigeonholing, Liszt obliterates the key signature and thus pays tribute, or so it seems, to C major, to which the motive migrates.

This debouches into a restatement of the principal subject in A-flat major. Capping it off is a vigorous A-flat major chord, prominently announced and followed by two and a half bars of a notably pregnant silence. Suddenly, a G-sharp minor chord bursts out of the silence, thus establishing itself as a Neapolitan relation to F-sharp major, which Liszt now restores. With the home key back in place, three chords—the tonic, dominant, and subdominant—combine and overlap in the final seven bars, bringing the work to its serene conclusion.

"Sunt Lacrymae Rerum/En mode Hongrois" (There Are Tears for Things/In the Hungarian Mode)

The fifth work of the set, "Sunt Lacrymae Rerum/En mode hongrois," is likewise a contemplation of death and is one of Liszt's most poignant compositions. Despite the work's grim ambience, its dedication to Liszt's former son-in-law and student, the pianist and conductor Hans von Bülow, was doubtless a sincere gesture of friendship rather than an underhanded compliment. The solemn introduction, rootless and unaligned to any specific key—though a case could be made for A minor—ponders a tense and uneasy melodic fragment in the bass that contains within itself an augmented fourth (*diabolus in musica*) and an open fifth.

A no-less-elegiac response some ten bars later, marked "più lento," throws a lean, single-voiced variant of the fragment into austere relief against intermittent harmonic punctuations in the bass. It's a painful theme, setting a mood of abject sadness, if not regret.

As the key signature morphs into four flats, thus anticipating what at first appears to be F minor, a brief ray of hope illuminates the compositional landscape with an ascending dotted motive in thirds. But even this is defeated when, only a few bars later, the right hand crosses the left and sinks earthily into the bowels of the piano, as if it were digging its own grave. Striking a low bass F, it oscillates in dotted rhythm with an even lower pitch, E-flat, which presides just a whole tone below it. Elsewhere, the left hand marches forward in a procession of minor chords in quarter-note motion. The music then drifts off into a perilous episode of wandering, harmonically rootless bass octaves in anticipation of the restatement of the opening fragment. A crushing, acerbic dissonance pits D-natural against C-sharp as an expression of its hopelessness; it is a brief but nearly cataclysmic moment, a forecast of annihilation and existential angst that cries out in agony.

And yet, with unexpected fervor, the clouds recede and the musical sun peers out, if only momentarily. The key changes to A major, already an indication of brighter things to come. Here a yearning variant of the F minor second subject takes hold, though it now unfolds at a somewhat slower pace, in quarter-note, half-note, and eighth-note motion. But it is not finished just yet; the figure repeats astride a restless arpeggiation in eighth-notes, only to drift off, through the bass, into a recall of the più lento theme of the work's opening.

"Marche funèbre" (Funeral March)

An impassioned ascent of octaves swells *fortissimo* from the bass en route to the sparse unison octaves that bring the work to its stark conclusion, which poses in alternation only two chords: an altered sixth (F-sharp major) and A major.

Liszt composed the "Marche funèbre" in 1867 in honor of Emperor Maximilian of Mexico. Maximilian, who was the thirty-five-year-old younger brother of Emperor Franz Joseph of Austria, had been installed by the French as the reigning monarch, only to be summarily shot by the Mexican republican army.

The work emerges from silence—a half-rest—with a rootless seventh chord in the key of F minor. Following two more (quarter) rests, it expands into a funeral procession of likewise rootless chords astride a dark tremolando in the bass. Some ten bars later, the turgid principal theme makes its entrance, again in the bass, as a troubled march of ascending and descending octaves. The mood is solemn, the textures spare; indeed, octaves in both hands rule the day as they give voice to the insistent dotted rhythms that move the work forward in continuous oscillations.

The middle section is leaner still. Here, Liszt reduces the texture to a single line, which is a lean variant of the principal theme, now turned into a quiet meditation or prayer in the alto register. It is only briefly harmonized, for a bar and a half, by the addition of two voices above.

An ascending octave episode ensues against relentless tremolando in the bass, which then takes over and culminates in *fortissimo*. The key migrates to F-sharp major as a clarion call of major chords drawn from the principal theme. The concluding sixteen bars are triumphant as they explore a parade of tonic and subdominant chords. The work ends optimistically in F-sharp major, thus contradicting death as the end of all things but suggesting that it might be only a beginning.

"Sursum Corda" (Lift Up Your Hearts)

This is the final entry of the *Années de pèlerinage*, and what a finale it is. Composed in 1877, it takes up where "Invocation" (from *Harmonies poétiques et religieuses*) left off and is in the same key, E major. Indeed, it is a paean to hope, inspired as it is by the injunction of the celebrant to the congregation at the Catholic mass as part of the opening dialogue to the preface of the Eucharistic Prayer. It is a prayer of thanks and consolation, which Liszt codifies in an ardent, if somewhat acidic, melody in rising stepwise motion. This principal theme is distinguished at its apex by an especially expressive intervallic leap of a minor seventh. Liszt expands the theme into octaves as it continues its sojourn astride a continuous string of repeated chords in the baritone and tenor registers. A triumphant, bell-like climax emerges in triple *forte*; to convey its power and clarify his intent, Liszt uses no fewer than four staves to distinguish its noble canto from the pulsating repeated chord accompaniment below.

A restless ascent of octaves moves upward to a cadence on the dominant. And just as in the "Marche funèbre," the final bars elaborate a rising and falling pattern of tonic and dominant chords in juxtaposition, and atop a vigorous bass tremolando, two bars at a time. "Sursum corda" closes triumphantly with four bars of repeated E major triads and, in so doing, brings the entire *Années de pèlerinage* to an exceptionally rich conclusion.

Liszt and the Music of Earth, Heaven, and Hell

In the autumn of 1830, Liszt, romanticism's torchbearer in the post-Beethoven era, embraced the Christian humanist doctrine of the Saint-Simonians. Henri de Rouvroy, the Comte de Saint-Simon (1760–1825) and the group's inspiration, had died only five years earlier on the heels of a suicide attempt. His vision of a benevolent collective dedicated to the restructuring of civilization captivated certain members of the intelligentsia but failed to take hold in the popular imagination. The Saint-Simonians' agenda appealed enormously to artists, including Liszt, as it envisioned the social role of art as central to a civilized society and viewed the artist as the secular equivalent of a priest. Though he was sympathetic to their social agenda and political thinking, Liszt disavowed any formal connection to their society; he was not a member. But in a show of support, he would on occasion perform at their meetings. Little did he know the profound effect that the socialist philosophy they espoused would have on him, as it shaped his social conscience and, to a significant extent, influenced his musical aesthetics.

In this ever-so-French ethos, which carried in it the seeds of past and future revolutions, artists and intellectuals, in collaboration with pragmatic industrialists, hoped to forge, in the spirit if not to the letter of Catholic ideology, a world of equity and fraternity. It was an attempt to reinterpret the French Revolution in the spirit of utopian socialism. The movement would drift into messianic cultism under the leadership of Barthélemy Prosper Enfantin and eventually be declared outlaw by the French government in 1832, but that evidently did not bother Liszt, who found inspiration in its mixed pantheistic and liberal political outlook.

Around the same time, the young and impressionable Liszt also discovered the progressive, humanist philosophies of Pierre-Simon Ballanche (1776–1847) and the Abbé Felicité Robert de Lamennais (1782–1854). Though Ballanche embraced dialectical thinking as the measure of his worldview, extolled revolution as divine, and, like the Saint-Simeonians, embraced poets as acolytes of change, he was in many ways a conformist; he declined to confront authority or put himself in any real danger by virtue of his political or intellectual agenda.

Lamennais, on the other hand, was a philosopher and ordained priest who ran afoul of the Holy See with his fervent advocacy of suffrage, freedom of the press, and, most significant, separation of church and state. After enduring the condemnation of Pope Gregory XVI, and the ensuing rift with the church, Lamennais retired to his estate in Brittany, La Chênaie, where he continued to write his treatises and poems, becoming a mentor to young intellectuals eager to sip at his wizened trough. It was here that Liszt, too, encountered him, in the summer of 1834, after professing his deep admiration for Lamennais's magnum opus, *Paroles d'un croyant* (Words of a Believer), Liszt was profoundly affected by Lamennais, who roamed his estate without pretense and in often in rags, sharing bits of wisdom and his shrewd critical judgment with his young visitor.

Indeed, it was here that the seeds of Liszt's aesthetics came into focus, giving rise to a musical outlook that would go on to shape much of his religiously inspired music. It was here, too, that Liszt embarked on the composition of his *Harmonies poétiques et religieuses,* a set of highly individual compositions inspired by the poetry of Alphonse de Lamartine, whom we shall meet in a moment.

If Ballanche's notion that progress, evolution, and social structures (the church, the family, the school) were the personification of God (a notion that diminished, ironically, the concept of Almighty to the level of a good old boy), then Alphonse de Lamartine (1798–1869), a diplomat turned poet, was for Liszt the high priest of such lofty aspirations.

Lamartine's poetry cycle *Harmonies religieuses*, which inspired Liszt's own musical setting of the same name, was more than an ode to the

Creator. It foreshadowed several burgeoning aesthetic philosophies, among them the artistic synthesis known as the "Gesamtkunstwerk"; the Russian symbolists' doctrine of correspondences; and, in the twentieth century, Aldous Huxley's *Brave New World*. Through his poetry, Lamartine legitimized the validity of mystical experience, or, as theologians would later call it, nature mysticism. From this perspective, harmony could be experienced as the unity of spirit with the phenomenal world; it was up to the artist, as the curator of human genius, to bring it to life.

Liszt's spiritual aspirations, tempered by his social conscience, never yielded to any monolithic point of view. Certainly the roots of his Catholicism ran deep and colored his approach to life and art from childhood to the day he died. Music for him was nothing if not the principal expression of his spiritual agenda. If he grappled with the liberal perspectives of men such as Lamartine (whom he met in the 1820s), Lamennais, Ballanche, and Saint-Simon, it was in an effort to inform his own multivalent perspectives on issues of mortality, sin, redemption, and, not least, character. Perhaps his resolve to enter the priesthood to take the minor orders in 1865 is indicative of the conclusions he came to in spite of the influence of his mentors, Lamartine and Lamennais. Their disputes and differences with the Catholic Church notwithstanding, Liszt came to embrace the traditions of an institution that, in his youth, he had legitimately questioned. Certainly, some years earlier, in 1859, the death by consumption of Daniel, his twenty-year-old son by Marie d'Agoult, bore down heavily on Liszt, as it did on the rest of his family. The extent to which this heartbreaking event might have sent him deeper into his faith is anybody's guess.

Let's survey some of the unique works that codify and combine Liszt's literary and spiritual aspirations.

Harmonies poétiques et religieuses, S.173 (Poetic and Religious Harmonies)

Though it had preoccupied him for some time, Liszt completed several of the pieces of his *Harmonies poétiques et religieuses* in 1847 while visiting his lover-to-be, the Princess Carolyne von Sayn-Wittgenstein, on her family estate in Woronince in Polish Ukraine. Carolyne, the work's dedicatee, was only ten years old at the time, and all agog over Liszt's glamorous presence. *Harmonies poétiques et religieuses* did not see publication until five years later, in 1852. It comprises ten pieces (some of which are surveyed here), matching the number of years old the princess was at the time of Liszt's visit, Listed in order, the pieces are:

"Invocation" (surveyed here)
"Ave Maria"
"Bénédiction de Dieu dans la solitude" (surveyed here)
"Pensée des morts"
"Pater Noster"
"Hymne de l'enfant à son réveil"
"Funérailles"
"Miserere, d'après Palestrina"
"Andante lagrimoso"
"Cantique d'amour"

Predictably, given its composer's penchant for transcription, not every piece within it was originally composed for solo piano. "Ave Maria," "Pater Noster," and the elegant "Hymne de l'enfant à son réveil" are transcriptions of earlier choral works. The frequently performed "Funérailles," which Liszt did write for piano, is a rhetorical tour de force that pits the most delicate melodic ambrosia against a force field of relentless octaves and is perhaps the most well known of these ten works, thanks to the attention that so many pianists have paid it in recital and on disc. "Cantique d'amour," the set's finale, is an opulent, earnest, and profoundly moving evocation of the heart, while the wanderlust of "Pensée des morts," the most provocative and forward-looking of the entire set, is distinguished by its asymmetrical rhythms and daring harmonic schemata. As one of Liszt's death pieces, its position in the *Harmonies poétiques* is doubly symbolic, as it embraces mortality and redemption. But that is no surprise, as death had long fascinated Liszt, not so much as a matter of morbid curiosity as it was a principle of spiritual contemplation.

"Invocation"

This introduces the set. It is orchestral in stature and concept, availing itself of the acoustic and sonorous potential of the instrumentarium it aspires to be. Shrewd pianists must make every effort to imaginatively convey something of the aura of the strings here, or the brass and woodwinds there.

But what exactly does it hope to invoke? Liszt prefaces the work with Lamartine's brief yet inspiring poem:

> Arise, o voice of my soul!
> With the dawn, with the night!
> Soar upward like a flame,
> Expand like the wind!
> Float on the wings of clouds,
> Mingle with the wind, with the storms,
> With the thunder, with the onrush of the tides!
>
> Arise in silence,
> Where, in the shadow of evening,
> The evening light sways
> When the priest extinguishes the incense burner.
> Arise on the edge of waves
> In profound solitude
> Where God reveals Himself in faith!
>
> (Translation by John Bell Young)

A steady stream of chords configured in triplets sets this majestic work sailing in the piano's baritone register. Liszt casts "Invocation" in E major and maintains the presence of the tonic, modified by a descent of passing tones in the bass, for a full four bars. The pace is steady, as much due to the of 3/4 time as much to the tempo, andante con moto. Here the principal subject, proceeding mostly in ascending stepwise motion, introduces itself in the alto voice. Just as Lamartine's poem suggests, it expands in vigorously accented quarter-notes astride the chordal pulsations underneath, alighting two bars later on a thick chord that combines the tonic and the dominant. As the harmonic texture thickens, the theme continues to grow in crescendo, cadencing some five bars later on a procession of octaves that outline the dominant. The unusually long eleven-bar phrase period manipulates or expands our perception of time. Following a pause modified within a fermata, Liszt repeats this material, fattening the chordal progressions yet again as he brings the melody up by an octave to the treble register. The key drifts in to C-sharp major, the work's submediant.

A mysterious stream of octaves on D-natural gives way to a dark descent in the bass, evoking, perhaps, Lamartine's dark night. The right hand, taking charge with octaves, plays a brusque iambic dotted figure that thrusts itself forward in *fortissimo* octaves. Liszt has already abbreviated the phrase period, organizing the materials in more conventional four-bar units. A transitional passage avails itself of the principal theme, now configured in imperious rising octaves. Intermittent arpeggiated chords, embraced by the left hand, articulate the weak second beats in the bass.

Now a new theme prevails, announcing itself boldly in D major. It is an arching procession of octaves in stepwise motion that shifts upward to E-flat major only two bars later. Here the right hand crosses the left and surveys a stepwise descent in the baritone register, before reiterating the earlier dotted iambic figure. Massive dominant seventh chords in D major, carried by the left hand, stream forth and are vigorously supported by three successive F-sharps played by the right.

Here a variant of the principal theme imposes itself in B major and is announced by a prolonged B major triad. Marked "grandioso," this second subject is nothing more than an imperious chorale that proceeds boldly in muscular chords that ascend fearlessly to a G-sharp doubled by octaves in the soprano register and also complemented by its doppelgänger in the tenor. An imperious round of descending octaves follows and falls again into a full-length B major chord. As the figure repeats, the tonality momentarily shifts to D-sharp before configuring itself yet again in B. The punishing tumult of descending octaves cadences on B and segues into a brief eighth-rest prolonged under the restful crown of a fermata.

Now the texture diminishes to a whisper, though the motivic material remains the same. Here, as earlier, Liszt engages the fundamental principles of thematic transformation: themes resurface constantly but, rather than being radically varied, elaborated, or ornamented, obtain to a wholly new character. Much can be said about this incoming B section, which in many ways resembles a development in sonata form. Here the second subject's machismo is emasculated; dispatched to the alto and soprano registers, it emerges again. This now wispy pastiche, evoking flutes and clarinets, vanishes into a quiet B major triad before resuming its business, now configured as a single melodic strand in the left hand. What only minutes ago were octave cascades have morphed into a delicate, even serpentine thread.

A few bars later, Liszt banishes the key signature of four sharps, throwing the work into C major, at least ostensibly. But the harmonic facts say something else: The prevailing tonality is now C minor. The music has drifted to the lower register and is led by the bass, which descends, not by note, in stepwise motion. This in turn gives way to a passage that is the musical incarnation of Lamartine's sputtering incense burner, its flame wavering and flickering. As the sepulchral bass line proceeds in a succession of two-bar phrases, its rising stepwise quarter-notes alighting every other bar on a dotted half-note, it is punctuated in the baritone register above by intermittent chordal puffs. These are the harmonic embodiment of the priest's gentle breaths.

The addition of a steady stream of eighth-notes materializes in the middle ground between the bass and the baritone, heightening the tension as the texture again begins to thicken. The figure again expands in crescendo but also in imitation as the two outer voices emerge one from another in a kind of motivic relay. Twenty bars later, with the onset of a broad climax, the four-sharp key signature is restored, suggesting the return of E major, but it is in fact B major that emerges victorious here. At last, Lamartine's mélange of wind, storm, tides, and thunder expresses itself in this magisterial new configuration of the principal subject, its ascent in thirds abutting a parade of fleshy chords and spacious octaves. It presses forward cumulatively to *fortissimo* under an unforgiving crescendo, the round of imitation between the left hand's octaves and the right hand's spacious chords not giving in for a moment. An immense climax on a dominant ninth chord in D major brings the passage to an abrupt, if powerful, half cadence.

Here the principal theme returns, much in the manner of the work's opening, but now considerably more insistent and as it roars in *fortissimo* above a continuous pulsation of combined subdominant and dominant chords. Together these form a prolonged pedal point, the antagonistic dissonances blending into a single, organ-like sonority. But the climax is extended to include a turbulent barrage of falling octaves that debouche into a variant of the iambic dotted motive of the opening's transitional material. Brazen leaps toss the octaves from one end of the keyboard to the other, alighting on two arpeggiated, rootless secondary dominants in the upper registers.

Suddenly, as if pushed from a precipice, the harmony drifts into a chromatic abyss; it is a transitional passage that slithers, in each successive measure, both upward and downward in stepwise motion. It swells steadily from *piano* to *fortissimo*, landing heavily on a fat dominant seventh of E major. The proud chorale reasserts its dominance with gusto as it gives way to rows of descending octaves between truncated restatements of the chorale. Octaves rule the day yet again as the left hand ascends from bass to treble astride a repetitive pulsation of tonic chords. Three E major chords, played in triple *forte*, bring *Invocation* to its bold, basso conclusion.

"Bénédiction de Dieu dans la solitude" (The Blessing of God in Solitude)

Like the other works in the set, Liszt prefaces "Bénédiction de Dieu dans la solitude" with Lamartine's poem:

> Whence comes, oh my God, this peace that overwhelms me?
> Whence comes this faith my heart is overflowing with?
> To me, who moments before, uncertain, agitated,
> And on the currents of doubt tossed by the four winds,
> Searched for the good, the true, in the dreams of the wise
> And for peace in hearts ravaged by storms.
> On my brow only a few days have slipped away,
> It seems that a century and a world have gone by;
> And that, severed from them by an immense abyss,
> A new man in me is born and starts anew.

(Translation by Eric Le Van)

The work, which Liszt casts in F-sharp major, a key he often assigns to music associated with either heaven or things beatific, begins without introduction. The principal theme, which swells up from the bass without fanfare, is a prayerful confection that extends over eight bars. Though approached by three descending notes, which form an upbeat, the melody itself proceeds in both stepwise and conjunct motion. The mood is calm and imperturbable as it floats easily from the dominant C-sharp in the baritone register to a C-sharp in the tenor above. Elsewhere, in the first our bars the right hand articulates a fluid two-voiced stream of eighth-notes: here, the alto register outlines an F-sharp major arpeggio while the soprano oscillates over two pitches, C-sharp and D-sharp. The pattern is repeated in B major in the fourth and fifth bars of the phrase.

For the pianist this is not so easy, as there can be no unwanted or un-indicated accents anywhere, and the passage requires, just as Liszt demands in his score, a seamless legato. The consequent phrase extends to ten bars as the theme exfoliates in the tenor range and breathes life into an endearing consolation. The second subject is another rising, prayerful invocation and is likewise modeled on the principal theme; it unfolds entirely in the tenor register astride a calming procession of eighths and a quarter-note motion in the bass.

A delicate wash of fourths and fifths prevails over eight bars en route to a restatement of the principal theme, which is now transferred to the alto voice. Now the two-voiced, double-note accompaniment emerges in the left hand as the melody unfurls itself in the right amid a patter of brief, harplike arpeggiations. As if to drive home a point, Liszt restates the melody yet again, expanding it further into an opulent array of broad arpeggios in the treble, and these segue into octaves upon the reemergence of the lyrical consequent. Extending the theme further, the key changes to B-flat major and then, only a few bars later, back to F-sharp major en route to a cadence on the dominant seventh, which coincides with a powerful, triple-*forte* climax.

Just as suddenly, the dynamic drops to *piano* and the opening thematic material returns. As the double notes drift and configure, within their texture, a succession of descending pentatonic scales, the work takes on an Oriental patina that adumbrates Debussy. A hypnotic procession of fourths and fifths purrs delicately in *pianississimo* and dissolves into a quiescent cadence on the tonic.

The ensuing middle section, marked "andante," gives voice to a simple, falling dotted motive in D major. If Liszt's objective was to convey contentment, rather than consternation, he succeeded here, codifying the peace that Lamartine extols in his poem. This interlude is brief and continues for only forty-five bars before hemorrhaging into a placid new episode in B-flat major, which Liszt is careful to mark "più sostenuto" (more sustained). A languorous variant of the principal theme sings out plaintively, not mournfully, in the tenor register. Its mood of resigned contemplation darkens and intensifies as it makes its way back to F-sharp major and a robust restatement of the principal theme.

Here the principal theme expands in broad chordal arpeggios in the alto and soprano registers as the left hands swings compulsively and continuously astride oscillations of oceanic arpeggios. The music reaches toward exaltation as it lurches into a sequence of thick chords that rise in stepwise motion and out of phase. The moment of climax in triple *forte* exudes an ecstatic reiteration of dominant sevenths in both hands. A cadence on the dominant does not dawdle but rushes headlong into a dazzling profusion of right-hand arpeggios, to which Liszt adds, only a few bars later, a fragment of the principal theme in the left. These culminate in a gossamer web of *pianissimo* arpeggios that rise and fall over a five-octave range.

An ad libitum consequent contemplates a series of broken chords before alighting on the coda, where Liszt slows the pace to andante. Here a reticent, wholly conciliatorily new theme emerges in the soprano register, and in four-part harmony, with an accompanying pulsation of eighth-notes. A recall of the drooping, kindly middle-section andante resurfaces for eight bars but is cut short, after its cadence, by a quarter-rest modified by a fermata. The concluding seven bars, embodied by a procession of chords in quarter-note motion, recapture the lyrical più sostenuto theme of the middle section. Sandwiched between the concluding tonic chords is a dominant, which draws the "Bénédiction" to its pious close.

Mephisto Waltz, No. 1, S. 514—*Der Tanz in der Dorfschenke* (The Dance in the Village Inn)

Of the four Mephisto Waltzes that Liszt composed between 1859 and 1885, only the third and fourth were written exclusively for piano. The first and second were originally orchestral works, which he only later transcribed, not only for piano solo, but for two pianos and piano duet, as well.

Liszt composed this, the first and most well known of Liszt's four Mephisto Waltzes (the fourth remained unfinished at the time of his death) between 1859 and 1862. He had just suffered the death of his young son Daniel a year before in 1858, and only two years later came the loss of a daughter, Blandine, in childbirth. Perhaps something of the trauma attached to those events convinced him that this decision to abandon the concert stage some years earlier, in favor of composition and the pursuit of a spiritual life, was the right one.

The work wastes no time in establishing its picaresque agenda. It was inspired by an episode from Nikolaus Lenau's (1802–1850) *Faust*. Liszt had intended to have its earlier, symphonic incarnation published and indeed performed alongside his *Midnight Procession* (Der nachtliche Zug), likewise a dramatic program music inspired by Lenau's *Faust*. Instead, they were published independently. Liszt, who often lamented the audacity of his publishers, who more often than not either refused or simply omitted to include in his scores the literary source material of his inspiration, was certainly relieved to know that at least the following description of the Faust episode was imprinted:

> There is a wedding feast in progress in the village inn, with music, dancing, carousing. Mephistopheles and Faust pass by, and Mephistopheles induces Faust to enter and take part in the festivities. Mephistopheles snatches the fiddle from the hands of a lethargic fiddler and draws from it indescribably seductive and intoxicating strains. The amorous Faust whirls about with a full-blooded village beauty in a wild dance; they waltz in mad abandon out of the room, into the open, away into the woods. The sounds of the fiddle grow softer and softer, and the nightingale warbles his love-laden song.

The Mephisto Waltz is a minefield of technical obstacles, which oblige the pianist to transcend them in favor of conveying both its rhetorical gestures and its poetry underneath. In more ways than one, the Mephisto Waltz brings to mind the music of Scarlatti: vast leaps, streams of unbroken scales, and sonorous arpeggios span the full length of the keyboard as angular rhythms, interlocking octaves, and intricate scale passages elaborate its facade. Punctuating all this is a yearning cantabile that empties graciously into a series of leggierissimo trills in thirds, followed by a diaphanous passage in the upper registers of the keyboard that evokes the song of a nightingale.

But behind this elaborate array is something more than mere display. Indeed, the Mephisto Waltz is nothing if not a story to be told. Its reservoir of gestures is hardly an occasion for superficial virtuosos technical display but an opportunity to harvest a wealth of affective nuance. This approach or attitude distinguishes, in the best performances, the pianist from the artist.

The work launches itself with rapidity in A major in 3/8 time, giving voice to an insistent pedal point on a single E-natural in the bass, which is modified once every six beats by an appoggiatura. Only four bars later, the procession of open fifths begins, as Liszt stacks a B-natural astride it. The progression of fifths continues for another eight bars before breaking into the rudiments of what will become the idée fixe of the entire work: a thematic survey of an open fifth that unravels as a two-bar theme in its own right.

Though the metrical organization is clearly three beats per bar in four-bar phrase periods, there is another, subtler way of objectifying the rhythmic (as opposed to merely metrical) trajectory here, which pianists will find especially interesting and useful. Rather than counting three beats per bar (which is objectively undesirable anyway, and for a conductor—either in the orchestrated version or in any piece that avails itself of a similar meter—impossible), one can hear a rather different pattern, though in eights: 1 2 3 / 1 / 2 3 / 1 2 3 4 5. In counting (or, really, feeling) this way through much of the opening (and, indeed, through much of the entire piece), the thrust of the ongoing rhythm assumes a cumulative continuity that is otherwise denied it. Granted, in such places it is most efficient—and effective—to avoid counting by beats at all, but instead in whole measures, wherein each bar is accorded a single beat. Counting in three eighths creates a tendency to accentuate the downbeat of every bar, which must be avoided in any case. Even so, pianists are well advised to experiment, and without making a meal of the aforementioned 3, 4, 5 pattern, to experience the rhythmic undertow that counting in this manner, at least initially, engenders.

Following a battery of parallel staccato octaves played with mischievous abandon by both hands, a fragment of that splayed open fifth of the opening emerges, but now transformed. While its rhythmic pattern of two eighths configured as an upbeat to a quarter-note is maintained, its intervallic dimensions have been diminished from fifths to thirds, with a minor sixth defining the leap over the bar line.

After an upward flourish of arpeggios astride yet another open fifth, the principal theme at last emerges in its full glory. It has expanded from two to eight full bars as it gives voice to a playful descending eighth-note pattern ornamented by a flurry of sixteenths, which are nothing more than ornaments—a turn, to be specific—that Liszt takes the trouble to write out, as opposed to leaving its execution to chance with its corresponding ornamental symbol. In so doing, Liszt asks the pianist to deny the figure any nimble-fingered superficiality but instead to convey its melodic attitude.

A cadence on an F-sharp triad in third position anticipates a temporary shift of key to A-flat major. Here Liszt elaborates the figure, toying with it as if to make a mockery of its character. Octaves leap and saunter in the left hand as the right engages a litany of scrunched appoggiaturas in a tight ascending sequence. This segues into a scintillating scale passage that rises to and falls precipitously from the piano's northernmost region, followed by a brilliant artillery of broken octaves. Here Liszt exacerbates musical tension by imposing a battery of alternating octaves that soon enough debouche into a massive glissando, and a restatement of the principal theme in octaves. Yet even here, in such razor-sharp passagework, savvy pianists, whose objective is to make music, not sound effects, have their work cut out for him.

A passage of massive chords, configured as duplets, momentarily interrupts the triple meter, which is restored soon enough by an ascending parade of octaves. The principal theme returns, reinforced by thickened chords. Petering out and gasping for breath, the figure abandons its chordal array and evaporates into a sparse trochee of only two notes played by the right hand and punctuated briefly in the left by condensed diminished chords and eighth-rests. The right hand throws out a slim chromatic oscillation of only two notes, E and D-sharp, which discreetly anticipates the ensuing B section.

With the introduction of the B section, Liszt slackens the tempo. The mood turns from imperious to languid as the principal theme undergoes a remarkable transformation. Liszt is careful to instruct the pianist to use the una corda pedal, thus muting the volume. A variant of the principal theme, now cast in D-flat major, morphs into a lyrical if disarming melody of halting syncopes configured into a distended melody, the individual constituents of which are cast on the third beat of each bar. As each of these harmonic systoles is suspended over the bar line, it ascends upward by a minor second and perfect fourth before descending again through a tritone. A minor and a major sixth articulate its denouement with a minor and then a major sixth, extending yet again over eight full bars. Following a varied repeat of this material, a dolorous dialogue of rising and falling perfect fifths pleads appealingly in slurred duplets.

Again, four bars of silence—which in through-composed music is never really that as much as it is music without notes—precedes an entirely new section. With a delicate trill of the seventh chord a certain diablerie materializes *pianissimo* in the upper treble. Its shimmering patina is like the play of shallow light that slices through the bony crevices of clattering skeletons. The texture has thinned to only three airily displayed voices. The B section's principal theme, itself a variant, emerges anew in octaves, but here transformed into a dreamy improvisation that is at once restrained and impassioned atop arpeggiated rotations below.

As if to drive home the fact that the Mephisto Waltz is yet another exercise in thematic transformation, much along the lines of the Sonata in B Minor, Liszt spreads the ensuing section over three staves. This serves not only to clearly delineate and make sense of its four voices, but, more pragmatically, to clarify the visual geography of the phrasing. Here a wispy array of repeated notes and broken octaves is entrusted to the right hand as the left, virtually accompanying itself, again articulates the lyrical syncopes in ascending sequences.

Despite the sparse texture that prevails throughout this eerie "un poco meno mosso," the challenge for the player here is to sustain its quiescent, nearly weightless ambience in a subdued *piano*. Intermittent swells give rise to gentle dynamic pulsations, indicated by hairpin crescendos. Liszt vaporizes the key signature some twenty-four bars before the section's end, not so much to throw the tonality into C major—which it most certainly is not!—but as a means to liberate, on a blank slate, the harmonic field from any specific key allegiance.

At long last, the principal theme of the A section returns in B-flat major, but now cast as a low and distant growl in the bass astride a tremolo-like rumble that lingers below. A chilly arpeggio, played by the right hand, disintegrates downward into a bold, metrically reorganized restatement of the now familiar syncope theme. The key migrates formally to A major as Liszt confounds our expectations by doing away with the syncopes entirely; what was once a waltz now assumes something of a marchlike character in 2/4 time. The theme, now entrusted to powerful octaves in the left hand, appropriates the strong beats, grounding itself as the right hand thrusts forward in a torrent of impressive arpeggios. On the heels of the intoxicating swirl of the arpeggios, the devil's orgy has only just begun.

And yet, for the entire textural thickening and the sudden stridency, Liszt asks for quiet. The dynamics move from *piano* to *mezzo forte* with intermittent sforzando punctuation. Yet these occur within an overall quiescent context, and even then, only at the top of the right hand's brusque arpeggiations. Liszt also proffers, with each rise and fall of the arpeggios, a crescendo and decrescendo, but this hardly means that the passage ought fall blithely into *fortissimo*; on the contrary, even here a discerning pianist will find opportunities to inflect the figure, carefully stringing it together within the context of a suave legato and a carefully adjudicated but gradual increase in volume.

But even on this occasion, cumulative energy is not static but fluid; this, too, is part of its specific intonatsiia. To be sure, each successive appearance of these broad arpeggios, which span more than three octaves on the keyboard, bears witness to greater intensity and snowballing dynamics. If there is one reason that Liszt's most virtuosic music continues to suffer to this day, is that unobservant, even insensitive pianists prefer to exploit precisely this sort of passagework as a means to show off. Certainly, in this poetry be damned approach, nothing works better for the crash-and-burn philosophy of piano playing than a ribald *fortissimo* and a furiously fast run.

Those who pay attention to Liszt's score will serve both the rhythmic trajectory and the spirit of the Mephisto Waltz well. Indeed, this entire passage, when evaluated within the larger context and in relation to what follows, is nothing more than a gigantic upbeat. Its meaning within the musical fabric becomes clearer when it is interpreted as a transitional passage en route to something or greater importance. Only in its last two bars, before the meter reverts to 3/8, does he intensify the volume with a più crescendo. Only six bars earlier, he inserted a "poco a poco crescendo," which indicates a gradual increase. But no crescendo, no matter its length or intensity, can be rendered perceptible unless it proceeds from a considerably quieter dynamic.

Thus when the A section's bold principal theme surfaces again on a decisive downbeat and in bright, soprano register octaves, something of a pinnacle has been reached. The left hand fleshes out this now renewed theme with exceptional vigor. It alights suddenly on a propulsive passage of merciless intensity that continues nonstop in rising chordal sequences for some twenty bars. The sharp, even electric alacrity of the passage might suggest, to those who are programmatically minded, a pitchfork, the three jagged eighths in each of these twenty bars akin to its prongs.

Unexpectedly, a full measure of silence intervenes, providing a frame for the next section, marked "presto." Motivically, this new section, a furious gallop of octaves in 2/4 time, reinvents the syncope theme, concealing it in diminution and simultaneously alluding to the puckish appoggiatura sequence of the A section. Though metrically organized as two beats per bar, its larger rhythmic impulse relies on Liszt's division of each beat into triplets, with the strong beat of each triplet entrusted unapologetically to the left hand. The excitement is palpable as it reaches its cadence in a feverish reversal, converting the triplets, without warning, into slurred chordal duplets in reminiscence of the A section's jarring close.

What follows is arguably the work's most celebrated passage, at least among pianists who either fear or welcome it. Neither posture will do, so long as it is played with the callous dispatch of those who favor mechanical brilliance over poetic intent. A consecutive series of long-limbed leaps in both hands articulates the syncope theme, now transformed staccatissimo—a rare instruction in any musical era—into something biting and sarcastic. That these unfold in an extreme tempo (presto) and, to make things even more difficult, in the context of a quiescent *piano*, makes for a kind of theater in its own right, at least visually.

But no one, least of all the performer, ought be seduced into believing that even this amounts to mere acrobatic panache for the soloist's benefit. Impressive though it is when played accurately, the passage still demands inflection, just as its slower and more languorous counterpart did at the beginning of the B section, of the most delicate variety. If all focus is placed on the leaps alone, thus giving undue emphasis to the upper partials of the right hand, any sense of the passage's shape and trajectory will be lost. Indeed, at least six voices are at work within this otherwise lean figure, and the destiny of each of them—that is, where they are going and their harmonic function—requires the interpreter's undivided attention.

It might be possible to fashion an interpretation of the first Mephisto Waltz that endows each passage with something of an upbeat character en route to that which follows it. From this perspective, the work would be all about cumulative energy. Thus, with the emergence of the last lusty throw of arpeggios, which well up like a wounded animal from the middle range of the piano, the game is up. As the left hand holds forth with no less ardency, the right hand lends its support with a pair of trochaic octaves, distended into slurred thirty-second-note couplets on every other downbeat, and then an urgent round of triplets that move passionately into deftly accentuated rootless ninth chords.

But what can the pianist do, you might ask, to draw out the poetic content of this presumably busy bit of virtuosity? What is it that, in a fast and furious (words that even Liszt himself was fond of using) performance of this well-worn work, we should look for, or should I say, listen for? After all, what's to be done with such a litany of arpeggios, which even the composer indicates are to be played triple *forte* and at such a swift pace?

The answer is: Plenty! The harmony holds the key here, as it has throughout the entire piece. But here the music benefits enormously if the constituents of the harmony outlined by each whooshing arpeggio are set forth with real vigor and definition. To that end, a particularly scrupulous pianist might engage and even emphasize, both dynamically and by means of a slight lengthening of these pitches, the first four notes of each arpeggio. The artist who gently emphasizes the dissonant relationships embedded within these arpeggios will go a long way to celebrating their implicit contradictions and the music's essentially ironic demeanor. Nor should the pulsating triplet chords in the left hand be marginalized as mere rhetorical bluster but instead should be boldly inflected.

As the octaves draw downward to a pungent close, an elaborate ornamental barrage ascends, in both hands, in stacked minor seconds and thirds. When it reaches an apex in the keyboard's stratosphere, it descends with equal fury, though now configured in diaphanous broken thirds and modified by a dramatic diminuendo. With that, a return to the skeletal remains of the B section's bony trill anticipates yet a new twist on the B section's seductive melisma. The harmonic texture is reduced to a single voice (the alto) and is occasionally punctuated with an arpeggiated chord. Representing the distant call of a nightingale is a stream of repeated high C's that debouche effortlessly into a twittering trill.

A blistering coda launches a fragment of the B section's syncope theme, which then blossoms into blustery, iambically configured chords. These give shape, for the very last time, to the same theme, its syncopes judiciously restored, though now in *fortississimo*. Evidently Liszt could not resist closing out the work in a sequence of brilliant interlocking octaves—one of the most impressive devices in the pianistic arsenal—in contradiction to an alternate, considerably quieter ending he penned for the orchestral version.

Mephisto Waltz, No. 3, S. 215a

A brief overview of the third Mephisto Waltz, which is seldom performed, is in order here, as it is a pivotal work in Liszt's overall musical output. Certainly, it is a wholly different affair from its cousin, the first Mephisto Waltz. Composed more than two decades later in 1885, it is among Liszt's very last works. In roughly twelve minutes it amply codifies Liszt's long-range artistic vision, which, for its audacious yet masterful flirtation with atonality, adumbrated the music of Scriabin as well as Schoenberg and the Second Viennese School.

This is not to suggest that the third Mephisto Waltz is a reservoir of tone rows or awash in retrograde inversions; it is not. Nevertheless, its opening fanfare moves marchlike through an unusual harmonic terrain. While this Mephisto Waltz has its detractors, who find its harmonic gestuary jarring, even its devotees sometimes misunderstand it. In *Guide to the Pianist's Repertoire* (Indiana University Press), Maurice Hinson, for example, characterizes it as redolent with a mood of cruelty, violence, and anger as "Liszt seems progressively to suppress and erase lingering traces of erotic tenderness."

While it is true that Liszt's aesthetic sensibility at this late period in his life had purged itself of any overt eroticism—such as the kind we encounter in the languorous middle section and the lusty finale of the First Mephisto Waltz—the Third Mephisto favors abstraction over program. Liszt, with characteristic humor, could be self-deprecating about this work. Upon hearing his student Clothilde Jeschke play it, he gave her some rather unusual advice. "I will tell you the review you will get if you play that in concert. It will say 'very talented young woman, a lot of technique! Only too bad she occupies herself with such terrible pieces. The composer truly seems never to have studied the rudiments of harmony and strict form. Certainly the opening already shows that!'"

In saying as much, Liszt was merely sending up the legion of critics, which is to say the overwhelming majority of them at that time, who would most certainly fail to understand what the piece was all about. Well aware that it would likely be long after his death before anyone, least of all critics, would be able to grasp it, he resigned himself to his fate with a sardonic wink of the eye.

Though the Faust legend again informs the spirit of the Third Mephisto Waltz, the music is no longer the stuff of theater or rhetoric, but of disembodiment. Liszt had long since embraced Catholicism as not only the definitive driving force of his existence, but as the inspiration (but not the compositional capital) for his aesthetic philosophy. What he attempts to codify in the third Mephisto Waltz is hardly cruelty and violence, as Mr. Hinson surmises, but spiritual exaltation. Of course, the music of Liszt, no matter its spiritual disposition or its hierarchical position in his compositional canon, always runs the risk of sounding like empty clatter. In this case virtuosity becomes a fetish for its own sake, or what Jankélévitch amusingly describes as "the idolatry of appearance and the regime of heavy make-up."

Even so, perhaps there is an opportunity to draw a structural homology of some sort, much as Richard Taruskin did so persuasively in *Defining Russia Musically* (Yale University Press), with regard to Scriabin. Can we surmise that the harmonic structures fashioned by Liszt, like those of Scriabin years later, not only represent the spiritual agenda to which they aspire, but quite literally embody those ideas? While this sort of investigation is best left to the musical semiologists, it nevertheless begs reflection. Does the piling up of tritones, for example, one upon another and in succession (as occurs in the third Mephisto Waltz), in some way, for their wholesale rejection of resolution and ambiguity, annihilate centrality and thus, by proxy, the musical equivalent of an ego formation? And is such selflessness, conveyed in purely compositional terms, equal to transcendence of the ego?

Whatever the case, with its concentration of tritones, whole-tone scales, and even occasional octatonic scales, Liszt's late-period harmonic ideology adumbrated that of Scriabin in more ways than one, and perhaps no more so than in the third Mephisto Waltz. If exaltation, then, has any site or substance in the music of Liszt, it is precisely in the context of such compositional tools and strategies. As we have already noted, the immanent ambiguity of the tritone, so perfectly proportioned as it divides a scale exactly in half, obliterates resolution and destabilizes tonality. Within this harmonic climate, where a specific, governing tonal center has been so thoroughly compromised, stasis reigns. Just as Scriabin would discern so shrewdly years later, it is precisely in exploiting this absence of centrality, the symbolic embodiment of ego, that Liszt establishes, in compositional categories, transcendence itself.

Impromptu in F-sharp Major, S. 191

Liszt penned the Impromptu in F-sharp Major in 1871, while in the midst of a most unfortunate episode with his near-psychotic piano student Olga Janina. Though she pretended to aristocracy, Olga was in fact the daughter of a shoe-polish manufacturer. Her ambitions and imagination got the better of her, compromising her judgment and behavior as she attempted to sully, with some success, Liszt's otherwise stellar reputation.

Today Olga Janina would be called a stalker. But for Liszt, she was something more: a gifted pianist and aspiring novelist who at first gained his trust and sympathy. She was sufficiently insecure to have taken grave offense at what she perceived to be Liszt's indifference, following his vigorous critique of a piano recital she gave in Paris; evidently, her concert, replete with memory slips, was a catastrophe.

Deeply hurt and intolerant, Janina went on to invent a tawdry fantasy that involved her nonexistent love affair with Liszt. Though it existed only in her mind, she flew into a rage when she felt the least bit slighted, and her dependence on drugs didn't help matters. After issuing a death threat against Liszt in the spring of 1871, she showed up unexpectedly at his digs in Budapest with a vial of poison and a gun. Suspecting she was suicidal at best, and homicidal at worst, Liszt calmed her, deflecting what could have turned into a very dangerous situation. Though the entire debacle might have been nothing more than a way to get attention, the incident riled him, and he resolved to get her out of his life.

Some years later, Janina took pen to paper in a biographical tome that painted Liszt as a nameless, mysterious "abbé"—a not-too-subtle allusion, given that just about everyone in Europe knew Liszt by that moniker. Though the book did Liszt no permanent damage, it certainly caused him some embarrassment. In any case, her smear campaign complete, Olga Janina vanished from Liszt's world and went on to spend her life as a piano teacher.

It was around the time of the F-sharp Major Impromptu's composition that Olga Janina cast a pox on his musical house. Fortunately, there was a kinder, gentler Olga in his life, an authentic aristocrat who had Liszt's best interests at heart. She also loathed Olga Janina. She was Olga, the Baroness von Meyendorff (formerly the Princess Gortschakoff). To this gracious lady Liszt dedicated the elegant, if rarely played, F-sharp Major Impromptu.

Introducing the work is an arpeggiated hover in F-sharp, which, entrusted to the left hand alone, unfolds in *pianissimo* triplets for two and a half bars. The lively tempo—"animato, con passion"—serves to enhance the work's weightless, disembodied hush. Almost imperceptibly, a simple F-sharp major triad in third position materializes in the alto register. Defying gravity, it stays put in gentle reiterations, five in all. Here the harmony migrates mysteriously, alighting for the next bar and a half on a derived dominant chord en route to an even more remote harmony, C minor. Such a kaleidoscopic shift of tonalities in such a short time span gives even Schubert a run for his harmonic money.

The texture thins as the right hand, standing alone, pipes out flute-like a gentle stepwise descent in whole tones. An airborne trill trails off into a F-sharp cadence. Liszt reprises the opening material, which he now expands into widely spaced chords, now in root position though no less quiescent, en route to the now familiar cadence. But here a diaphanous spray of sixteenths drifts southward to a new cadence on the dominant.

Although the hovering pulsation of rotating triplets presses on, an ominous new melodic fragment emerges in the bass, played by the right hand, now discreetly crossed over the left. This brief but lightly ornamented theme orbits around a C-sharp, the dominant of the F-sharp but also the tonic in this new tonal context. A chromatic ascent to D-natural, the sultry Neapolitan, rides astride the river of triplets, which have likewise morphed to D minor. The melodic fragment, only moments earlier the provenance of the bass, ascends angelically to treble in octaves. Below it, the roaming triplets of the left hand assume the status of a contrapuntal melody as the first notes of each triplet are deftly articulated and linked, one to the other, in an ambling melodic line all their own. The figure's wanderlust is palpable as it meanders towards the brighter harmonic regions, alighting in D major in the piano's stratospheric treble.

With this the principal subject returns, now broadened into fleshy chords in the right hand while the triplet pattern, again reinforced by a descending melodic pattern in octaves, crescendos to *fortissimo*. As the texture thickens, the figure segues into an ecstatic rhythmic profusion of six beats per bar. D major evaporates, as does its key signature, making room for the new tonality, C major.

Now Liszt has taken us to a key that lies at the distance of an augmented fourth from the home key of F-sharp major; it is our old friend the *diabolus in musica*. But here, a C major triad oscillates periodically with an A major chord, thus emphasizing the relation of their respective scalar constituents, C-natural and C-sharp. The mood is one of heartbreak, even desperation, as if the theme, truncated and unfulfilled, has been banished from its realm, its final peace denied it. It is, in effect, an existential scream, from a once vibrant but now wizened entity denied a resolution as its purpose is compromised.

We can only wonder if Liszt discerned or actually cites the pivotal harmonic strategy that defines Schubert's "Wanderer" Fantasy, as well as his lied "Der Wanderer"—both works that Liszt knew well and adored. Indeed, the extraordinary "Wanderer" Fantasy exerted a profound influence on the young Liszt, so much so that he transcribed it for piano and orchestra. The juxtaposition of these two pitches, which orbit one around the other ad infinitum throughout both "Wanderers," represents Schubert's "Fremdling" (stranger), a symbol of alienation and death. Their relationship coincides with Georg Schmidt von Lübeck's chilling text: "Die Sonne dünkt mich hier so kalt, die Blüthe welk, das Leben alt, und was sie reden leerer Schall . . . Ich bin ein Fremdling überall" (The sun seems so cold to me here, the flowers faded, life old, and what they say has an empty sound . . . I am a stranger everywhere).

Resigned to a fate that only posterity would judge, Liszt may have intuited in this haunting impromptu his very own Fremdling, that is, the alienation he felt but nobly endured to his last breath. Despite his celebrity, Liszt, like Schubert, was sorely aware that his extraordinary compositional achievements would likely be denied recognition in his lifetime. How right he was.

A distant trill vibrates on a high C-natural and D-flat, bringing things to cadence above a C major arpeggiation. A ghostly roulade in sixteenth-notes descends onto a plank of open and augmented fifths before F-sharp major reestablishes its primacy. But now the triplets are nowhere in sight. The harmonic rhythm slows tonic and arid, rootless dominants, in a chromatic procession, resign themselves to their fate. A dominant pedal on F-sharp tolls *pianissimo* in the bass below, but its sepulchral authority is attenuated by the conciliatory demeanor of the shifting harmonies above. The mood is serene, the musical atmosphere crepuscular. The concluding eight bars pay tribute to an impressionistic, wholly transparent progression of chords in parallel motion that drift downward from their celestial perch to rest on two quiescent F-sharp major chords that it desperately sought.

Ballade in B Minor, S. 171 (CD Track 4)

Though Liszt composed the Ballade in B Minor in 1853—the same year as the B Minor Sonata—it refers back to an event some four years earlier. Though this second of his two ballades has no specific program attached to it, the fact that Liszt dedicated it to Károly Leiningen is significant. In 1849 the Hungarian uprising—what some have termed a revolution, and which would be repeated in more ways than one more than a century later—depended on the commitment and advocacy of thirteen brave Hungarian generals men to keep its fires stoked and the Hungarian people informed. These men were scions of Hungary's aristocratic families, and the execution in October of that year of all thirteen of them certainly called into question the idea of justice in that troubled land. Only a year earlier, Liszt had already lost one friend, Prince Felix Lichnowsky—whose family had patronized Beethoven only fifty years earlier—to mob violence. Thus the dark clouds of revolution and tragedy were very much on Liszt's mind when he dedicated this work to his friend the Count Károly Leiningen.

Program or not, this work symbolically tests an assumption of heaven, and perhaps hell, too; but it most certainly evokes the quotidian realities of earthly conflicts. It begins with a mighty rumble, a rolling oscillation of rising and falling chromatic scales in the burly bass. The mood is dark, cloudy, and oppressive. An autumnal melody in the baritone voice lurks above, its anxiety driven by its upward trajectory in stepwise motion.

A brief but impassioned tag swells up in solo from the bass, en route to a cadence on a lone C-sharp—a constituent of the dominant. This bit of preparation introduces a new theme, the significance of which in this work cannot be underestimated. It is a slow (lento assai) and plaintive chorale, which Liszt elaborates and accelerates in a curvaceous extension, marked "allegretto," astride an array of dominant chords. Following an identical repetition of the material in B-flat minor—at the distance of only a half step below—a new section ensues.

It would be easy to impose on this work, as some do, something akin to sonata form, and indeed, to do so would not necessarily be wrong. But if Liszt deliberately appropriated the formal conventions of the classical period, he did so without dwelling on the exigencies of the form. Liszt was, in his dramatic music, of which the Ballade in B Minor is certainly representative, considerably more fluid than that.

Even so, the martial theme that inaugurates this new section, marked "allegro deciso," marches forward atop a brief battery of repeated octaves. Whereas the opening was in 6/4 time, this episode, taking its cue from the previous chorale, proceeds in the more resolute 4/4. Within moments the theme expands into an orchestral tutti of sorts, where a rat-tat-tat run is framed by a belligerent sequence of chordal triplets. Vigorous and largely diminished chord arpeggios sweep downward atop thick and dissonant chordal protrusions, alighting on heaving syncopes in the baritone register. The tempo heightens again to an intensely woven agitato, and in the right hand a patch of broken octaves streams upward in a liberal variant of the opening chromatic scale. The sea of sighs into which this figure expands profits from the litany of slurred and heavily accented chords that keep it moving and curry favor with harmonic tension.

Iambic fragments sputter loudly in successive leaps between the middle and upper registers, a codified (some would say clichéd) reference, perhaps to the more natural phenomenon of thunder and lighting. Here an ardent new theme, loosely based on the Allegretto that follows the chorale, unfurls itself in the alto and soprano registers. This elegiac line is pure vocalism, an homage to the deft elaboration of a *lirico spinto*; Liszt makes no bones about it conceptual origins, either, marking it "piacere cantando" (singing at will). Its anxiety proceeds from passionate concern, making the sunlight of what follows all the more poignant. Liszt again proves himself a master of monothematic transformation by elevating, if not so much transforming, the character of the sinewy Allegretto into an expression of beatific enchantment. As the tonality shifts into D major, Liszt extends the figure into a transparent chordal procession in the upper register of the piano. It coasts seamlessly astride a gentle lull of rolling triplets in the tenor and a bell-like pedal point in the bass and is a figure that for Liszt may well have represented the Eternal Feminine.

As it shores itself up for repetition, this heavenly episode shifts gears and moves into related tonalities of G major and C major. But a transitional passage briefly touches on E-flat major when suddenly a familiar grumble below proffers a return of the chromatic passagework of the beginning. A variant of the opening chromaticism again rears its head as the right hand streams in yet again with a swell of chromatic broken octaves. The left hand then takes over, assuming the broken octaves while the right lingers over the chordal harmonizations that punctuate it. Even now, Liszt cannot resist a thrilling effect: a woeful episode in descending interlocking octaves runs headlong into a powerful recall of the martial triplets of the Allegro deciso, ornamented and framed, as it were, with artillery blasts of interlocking octaves in the bass below. These in turn culminate in a bit of fiery of bravo, where interlocking octaves again rule the day as they pummel into a chromatic scalar descent in unison.

A fragment of the Allegretto theme informs the following passage, which seems to plea in earnest for something. The "piacere cantando" theme returns but is now cast in B major. The gentle Allegretto returns, too, though now Liszt deliberately alternates its chordal constituents between the hands, as if to create an internecine dialogue in unslurred duplets. The key migrates to E-flat and then back to B major as this now familiar fragment rotates upon itself en route to a brand-new theme, marked "cantabile"; it is an elegy that swells up in earnest and with autumnal assurance in the baritone register. Surrounding this appealing and wholly vocal profusion is a halo of eighth-notes that drift into rests, thus allowing the continuous tenor line to shine through on its own. As the theme then expands into octaves, the accompanying halo shifts into a flurry of ascending triplets.

A segue into a now impassioned and texturally expanded recall of the cantando piacere draws on the occasion to heighten both rhythmic and dynamic tension within the context of a crescendo and accelerando. The cantabile theme returns here but is now cast in fat *fortissimo* chords, played by both hands, while a brief whoosh of ascending and descending scales enriches it in the bass; in other words, Liszt combines the design, if not the chromatic-inflected letter, of the opening with the principal thematic material of this final episode. With that done, the cantabile theme repeats again, one last time, and is again given over to expressing itself in thick chords. But here Liszt expands the scale passage, now in ascent only, over a five-octave span from the baritone register to the upper treble.

A massive arpeggio spreads its wings as it hurls itself into a procession of syncopated ascending octaves, accompanied below with an ascent of chromatic sixths. These in turn segue into a bold parade of octaves played in contrary motion, as if Moses were parting the waters a with his magical staff as he intones his famous lines "Behold His mighty hand . . . Go, proclaim liberty throughout the land, and to all the inhabitants thereof!" This strikes me as an apt metaphor for this work, which was most certainly inspired by aforementioned tragic events in Hungary. A recall of the Allegretto motive breathes its last here in succession, until it finally collapses onto an E major triad and then finally onto the work's three concluding chords.

Inexperienced pianists, or those unfamiliar with Liszt's idiosyncratic compositional vocabulary—and its sources—might easily buckle under the temptation to show off the litany of roulades, double notes, and interlocking octaves that were so typical of his early and middle periods. Informed players, on the other hand, will keep the fervency and trajectory of the music in sight. The opening chromatic scales that rumble persistently through the bass, for example, are often played with a continuous pedal, which Liszt's own pedal markings would at first glance appear to support. But Liszt's pedaling, unlike Chopin's (which is more often than not pristine and precisely drawn,—which is not to imply it ought to be followed slavishly, either!), must not be taken literally. Its intent is invariably suggestive and flexible, and not necessarily structural.

Those who go after an effect by using long, unbroken washes of pedal to convey murkiness may labor under the impression that danger and foreboding are best conveyed in this manner. Indeed, the amusing but apocryphal notion that Liszt's inspiration for the ballade was the Hero and Leander myth, in which lovers, separated by tragedy, end up drowning in the Hellespont, contributes to legitimizing such muddy pedaling.

But given Liszt's embrace of the mysteries of Catholicism when he wrote the ballade, and particularly in light of its dedication to fallen heroes, I am inclined to think of the work as a kind of Passion play, a musical march, if you will, to Golgotha. It is no accident that Liszt punctuates long stretches of chromatic scales with chorales and hymns. Even the ethereal harmonizations over widely spaced, nocturnal arpeggios in the D major middle section, or the declamatory laments of the final pages, where ascending double scales lift to the top (as Arrau described it) as an unmistakable symbol for ascent, suggests a spiritual agenda. What lends this and the related recurring chromatic-scale passages their relentlessness is an undulating rhythm supported by dovetailing crescendos and decrescendos. And to create the impression of beatific detachment, or dreaminess, some degree of metrical precision is indispensable. Thus what Maria Callas and Conchita Supervía brought to bel canto singing is what the pianist must do here: shape and follow the contours of the counterpoint, emphasizing its salient points and throwing other material into the background (or middle ground).

Hungarian Rhapsody, No. 19, S. 244

In the rich and varied world of Franz Liszt and his music, a little hearsay has always gone a very long way. Take the case of the Hungarian Rhapsodies, which gave generations of pianists and listeners so much joy, the critics a great deal to complain about, and, for decades, the Hungarian people a reason to feel insulted. But whatever one thinks of them, the Hungarian Rhapsodies were for Liszt the music of *his* earth, an emblem of a culture to which he felt, by virtue of birthright and heritage, spiritually connected.

Liszt composed fifteen Hungarian Rhapsodies between 1847 and 1853, though these include an alternate version of the famous *Rákóczi March*. But even this series, which would eventually become the standard, was not the first; availing himself of many of the same motivic fragments that inform the final version for piano, Liszt had composed their progenitors as early as 1839, assembling them into a set of twenty-one pieces titled *Hungarian Themes and Rhapsodies*. These were published between 1840 and 1847. But even then, he wasn't finished with them. In 1874 he transcribed no fewer than six of these rhapsodies for orchestra (Rhapsodies 2, 5, 6, 9, 12, and 14) before writing four entirely new works in the genre, again for piano solo, in the last four years of his life.

Inspired by his 1840 visit to Hungary, where he had not set foot for more than sixteen years, Liszt embarked on a substantial project, which, though it did not quite attain to the level of scholarship, proved a significant contribution to music in general, and most certainly to his own work. He set out to gather the indigenous folk tunes of the Hungarian Gypsies, and he had them published in 1846 in several volumes titled *Magyar Dallok*, or Hungarian National Melodies. This in turn informed his decision to write an extensive critique of these melodies, which was later published in 1859 in two volumes as *Des Bohémiens et de leur musique en Hongrie* (The Gypsies and Their Music in Hungary). Actually, Liszt originally had only intended to write a brief preface for the Hungarian Melodies volume, but it mushroomed over the years into something far grander.

Gypsy life and culture had long captivated, since his youth in Hungary, Liszt's florid imagination. Indeed, he was convinced that the natural proclivities the Gypsies demonstrated for the musical arts was God given; how was it, he wondered, that these simple folk with a bad reputation could so fluently and fluidly churn out one exotic melody after the other and, what's more, give voice to those tunes with such highly charged feeling on their favored instruments, the violin and the cimbalom? The extravagance of the harmonic colorations, the improvisatory vivacity of the rhythms, the ornamental effusiveness of the passagework enthralled him to no end.

In coming to grips with the music of his native land, he came to envision this music not as a collection of isolated melodic fragments, but as an emblem of an entire culture, indeed, as a kind of epic poetry in sound, as if their music was a collective edifice, the historic dimensions of which were at once heroic and prophetic. He was touched and impressed by the seemingly natural abilities of the otherwise uneducated Gypsies to create such extraordinarily original music and to convey it with such freewheeling virtuosity. The now ebullient, now mournful qualities of this music evoked something of Liszt's own nomadic sensibility, which he shared in common with Gypsy culture.

But upon the publication of *Des Bohémiens*, Liszt was caught by surprise. The book caused an uproar in Hungary, where his peers and the critics, thoroughly indignant, condemned it and Liszt himself. It seems that even in Hungary, the establishment viewed the Gypsies as outsiders, as itinerant thieves and con artists who could not be trusted and who, in any case, given their rootlessness, were not authentic Hungarians. This was brazen nationalism by those who failed to appreciate either the role played by Gypsy culture in Hungary or the fact that so many of them were born there.

Liszt made the unfortunate political faux pas of attributing, in his book, the indigenous music of Hungary—which is to say, all of it—to the Gypsies. Although there was some truth in his assertion, the credit was in fact misplaced, as much of what Liszt intuited and, indeed, recorded in his book were either native Hungarian folk tunes or melodies composed by minor Hungarian composers. The Gypsies often appropriated this music and, like Liszt himself in his operatic transcriptions, made it into something of their own. Liszt's research into Hungarian music, then, rested entirely on his assumption that all the folk music he heard performed by Gypsies while he was in Hungary was in fact their own. Thus the Hungarian intelligentsia found Liszt's failure to distinguish one cultural genre from the other—no matter that one was influenced by the other more often than not—deeply offensive.

Not until Béla Bartók, who was no great fan of Liszt, came to his defense some seventy-one years later, in 1931, was Liszt's reputation in Hungary restored.

But even the work of as esteemed an authority as Bartók was unable to persuade Liszt's detractors in the twentieth century as to the musical value of the Hungarian Rhapsodies, which have alternately been dismissed as banal or disparaged as nothing more than virtuoso pandering. To make matters worse, the second rhapsody, hardly Liszt's magnum opus, became an object of popular idolatry in the cinema and, for years, in the concert hall; scarcely any pianists in the first half of the twentieth century failed to use it as a vehicle for showing off their skill in passagework, or to subject it to further elaboration, as Vladimir Horowitz did, for example, with devilishly difficult scales, octaves, and blistering roulades.

The immanent characteristics of so-called Gypsy or "Zigeuner" music, no matter its etiology, are various. Indeed, there is not nor has there ever been a single Gypsy culture, but instead it consists of innumerable clans, which have called Europe, the Near and Middle East, and even America their home. As we have seen from Liszt's efforts, which were justifiably if perhaps prematurely criticized by his colleagues, the Gypsies assimilated the music of whatever region they inhabited and made it their own. What has come to be known as the Hungarian Gypsy scale—whole step, half step, augmented second, half step, half step, augmented second, half step (C, D, E-flat, F-sharp, G, A-flat, B, C)—was a product of the nineteenth century and remains to this day the most widely recognized scale. What's more, the Gypsies appropriated two popular Hungarian dances: the *csárdás* (czardas) and the *verbunkos*. The former is a rapid, unusually intense confection in duple meter that had become all the rage in the 1830s, and the latter, which originated in the eighteenth century, involved two contrasting sections, the first a slow introduction (dubbed *lassú*), the second a fast and spirited consequent (*friss*).

Still, the Hungarian Gypsies have become, over centuries, most closely associated with an idiomatic sort of music known for its free-wheeling exoticism, as well as for a style of playing that is at once improvisatory and extremely expressive. The typical Hungarian Gypsy ensemble was traditionally made up of two violinists, a cimbalom player, and a double bassist.

If Liszt appropriated anything of value from the musical culture of the Gypsies, it was an approach to both sound and style that became, for the nineteenth century, an inimitable trademark. The wild, unbridled acrobatics of Gypsy violin music, with its profusion of string slides and elisions, was for Liszt's ears nothing less than ambrosia. Thus it was not only the celebrated violinist Niccolò Paganini, who took Europe by storm in the 1830s, whose virtuosity inspired Liszt, but also the Hungarian Gypsies with their idealized freedom from either technical or musical constraints.

The improvisatory elements of both the music and the manner in which the Gypsies presented it gave the young Liszt an idea: that the piano itself held for the artist likewise unbridled potential. With the Hungarian Rhapsodies and several sets of études, Liszt virtually reinvented pianism, entwining the conventional vocabulary of musical composition with the physiology of the pianist and the topographical physiognomy of the piano itself. Suddenly, with Liszt all manner of physical difficulty became not only acceptable, but a mode of musical expression in its own right. That this approach to both concept and composition stuck some of his more eminent colleagues as crude and even antimusical is not surprising, given the European musical establish disdain of Gypsy culture as anything worthy of serious artistic consideration. That said, the ensuing dispute over musical aesthetics that pitted the so-called absolutists (most notably, Brahms and Schumann) against those who advocated the supremacy of musico-dramatic forms and program music (Wagner and Liszt) was, under the circumstances, predictable.

The nineteenth Hungarian Rhapsody, in D minor, falls into two Lisztian categories: that of the genre from which it takes its name, and also that of the music from Liszt's late period—which is to say, his old age. He composed it in 1885, just a year before his death.

Its mood is at once solemn and mysterious as the slow introduction (the Hungarian *lassú* or *lassan*) articulates a slim chromatic oscillation, in the alto register atop double thirds, that segues into an ascending Gypsy scale. But its Zigeuner pretensions don't end there. A parade of descending unisons in rapid thirty-second- and then sixty-fourth-notes occupies five bars before landing squarely again on the *lassan*, now appropriated by the piano's tenor. Here the opening motive morphs into double sixths and harmonized octaves before a descending tumble of thirty-seconds emerges en route back to the *lassan* theme.

The pace hastens with breathless intensity in nervous five-note sequences that segue yet again into an impassioned plea of the *lassan* motive. The thirty-second-note motive returns again, but now configured as gossamer double thirds in the uppermost register of the piano. A diaphanous diminished chord unfolds as an ascending arpeggio, emptying itself into silence in anticipation of the *lassan*'s return.

At last, the *friska* (or *friss*)—the Hungarian term for the swift-tempo consequent—emerges in a sequence of punchy two-bar phrases defined by rising left-hand octaves and breathy chordal syncopes in the right. Soon enough it catches on fire as Liszt challenges the pianist to spin out with consummate energy and crystalline lightness a string of sixteenth-note arpeggios. The harmonic rhythm, too, increases as the sixteenths unfurl themselves chromatically, alighting on a triple-*forte* procession of diminished chords. A deft variant of the opening of the *friss*—wherein the oscillating sixteenths replace the octaves in the left hand—precedes leaping broken octaves in the right hand punctuated by tenths in the left.

The coda is nothing more than a variant of the *friska* theme, but now restated entirely in staccato double octaves and in D major. The pace swells from fast to feverish as the octaves give way to a certain exaltation that belies the usual methodology that defined much of Liszt's late piano music. Gone is the sparse (though not severe) texture, as if in fashioning this work Liszt wanted to pay one last homage to the virtuosity of his youth. The octaves segue into an insistent presumption of fat chords, which, for their designation in triple *forte*, betray a certain stridency as they march forward two to a bar for the next and final forty-five bars. An onrush of D major chords ascends, one per bar, through the concluding dozen measures, separated only by a quarter-rest in each bar. Though the concluding note is indeed a D, Liszt is careful to draw his ending on a full bar of silence, atop which he places a fermata. Savvy pianists will telegraph that silence on the heels of the final pitch, which is only the penultimate gesture, in any number of ways: by not removing their hands from the keyboard, or, on the contrary, by lifting them, in such a way as to create visually the sense of something yet to come. Such is theater in the piano music of Franz Liszt.

5 Operatic Paraphrases and Song Transcriptions

If opera was the nineteenth-century equivalent of contemporary cinema, the concert paraphrase was the television miniseries. The great theaters of Europe—La Scala, Covent Garden, the Paris Opera—were accessible enough to wealthy bourgeois patrons who, year after year, turned out in droves, tuxedoed and bejeweled, not only to hear the newest operas, but also composers' most fashionable new melodies.

With the development and popularity of the touring virtuoso/composer, as exemplified by Franz Liszt and Niccolò Paganini, opera became available to anyone with a piano. By then the piano was by and large fully developed, not appreciably different from today's modern instrument, and it rivaled the orchestra in popularity.

Through the art of transcription, or paraphrase, whole symphonies, arias, and overtures, now appropriated for the piano, could be played at home. In the concert hall, audiences looked forward to such works performed with virtuoso abandon and bravura by skillful soloists. For the average music lover, the paraphrase provided what recordings do today, with one major difference: the intimacy and personal satisfaction, nowadays but a fading memory, of making music at home with one's family. Thus, at the dawn of the industrial revolution, the transcription had come a long way from Bach's settings of hymns and cantatas.

Though it may be ill-advised to blithely think of the *paraphrase* (or *fantasy*) and *transcription* as interchangeable terms, they all refer to arrangements of the music of others. In the end, what really matters is the manner and success of his manipulation of the operatic, vocal, and symphonic music of his contemporaries and predecessors into wholly autonomous works for piano.

In his early paraphrases, such as the *Rigoletto paraphrase de concert* (Paraphrase on Themes from Rigoletto) or the monstrously difficult *Réminiscences de Don Juan* (Don Juan Fantasy), Liszt took the principal themes of the original work and embellished them with material of his own. They became, in effect, ideal vehicles for improvisation and variation. When the work is expertly performed, the results can be overwhelming; the music becomes nothing less than a "Technicolor" extravaganza. Thalberg dazzled his audiences, in his own paraphrases, with the so-called three-hand effect, wherein alternate, contrasting melodies were deftly embedded between the hands, weaving in and out of arpeggio cascades and mercurial, lightning-swift scales. Thalberg's efforts in the genre, largely forgotten and rarely played today, were eclipsed and rendered cliché by Liszt's ingenuity, which appropriated the very same effect, but to far greater advantage and musical purpose.

As a genre, the paraphrase was certainly nothing new, having grown out of a tradition that reached back as far as the fourteenth century. Composers were often asked by their publishers, or gave in to the demands of an adoring public, to transcribe their works, especially orchestral and chamber music, for piano. This practice allowed the average consumer, living in rural or less populated areas with limited or no access to concert life in major urban centers, to become familiar with themes that were seemingly on everyone's lips. In an era when neither recordings nor high-speed transportation existed, transcriptions made it possible to belt out on a keyboard the endearing tunes and inspiring rhythms of a Beethoven or Mozart, no matter how compromised those often neglected, out-of-tune rural instruments might have been.

While this was most certainly a productive development that made it possible for the general population to cultivate at least some knowledge of and, more important, love for great music, it also had a downside. Many composers penned transcriptions as yet one more means to make money. Others, like Beethoven, disdained the practice, at least where their own music, transcribed by anyone other than themselves, was concerned. Beethoven admitted his distaste for the genre, even though he himself penned a transcription of one of his early piano sonatas for a string quartet, as well as his Second Symphony for a piano trio.

So why, given the widespread acceptance and even the usefulness of transcriptions—as opposed to the more liberal, improvisatory fantasy or paraphrase—is a conductor or an orchestra even necessary? Why can't a great symphony, such as Beethoven's Fifth, be performed in its transcribed form by a competent pianist or a skilled chamber ensemble? What difference does it make, and wouldn't the music, in its new clothing, so to speak, exert the same effect on its listeners as the original? After all, music is music, and the pitch and rhythm material are identical in both versions, even if the instruments are not.

Well, the answer is simple. Things are not at all the same. The net effect of a piano transcription on our way of listening, that is, the manner in which we relate to the music itself, is an entirely different experience. The affective stimulation that only an orchestra can provide, on the other hand, fuels our emotional response to musical experience; a piano reduction—and make no mistake, that is precisely what it is, a reduction—remains wholly unsatisfactory in comparison.

These worthy, and certainly useful, transcriptions cannot in any way convey the immanent character of the instrumentation or the complexity of the orchestration. To be sure, as we begin to study these works in earnest, we realize these elements are not merely material properties but artistic ones, just as carefully adjudicated by composers (and interpreters) as the notes and rhythms they set to paper. They are in fact indigenous to the music itself.

When these works are played on the piano, we miss the ardency of the strings as they swell or diminish; we long for the plaintive reediness of a single, lonely oboe, the breathy vivacity of a flute, and the menacing vibrations of the timpani. The shimmer of a vibrato or the airy aspiration of a distant horn call cannot be effectively duplicated (though they might be suggested) with octave tremolos and pedaling tricks. Thus, in the absence of the spirited interplay of parts and instrumental colors, far too much gets lost in the translation. While it is an ambitious and tempting challenge for a pianist to live up to all that, it is quite impossible, as it is largely by virtue of the instrumentarium, made whole by the music, that something far more powerful and intimate stands to be realized by an orchestra.

Even Glenn Gould, who often carried off performances of piano transcriptions with unusual aplomb, could not rescue Liszt's transcription of the Fifth Symphony, in his otherwise fascinating recording, from its essential banality. That much is obvious. A piano is a piano, after all, and no matter how imaginative the pianist or how luxurious the instrument, it is, in the end, not a collection of violins and cellos, oboes and clarinets, trumpets and timpani, but a large box wired with strings, the sound of which diminishes almost immediately upon striking them. What's more, the tone quality of a string or woodwind instrument, while something a particularly savvy pianist may be able to imaginatively convey if not duplicate, is unique. Each is imbued with its own special color and, when combined with other instruments, attains to a synthetic timbre the quality of which is incomparable.

Here we will take a look at one of Liszt's admittedly more well-known operatic transcriptions, Isolde's "Liebestod" from *Tristan and Isolde*, as well as one of his more endearing transcriptions of a Schubert song, "Ave Maria." That I do so is not to dismiss by any means, his greatest paraphrases, namely those on Mozart's *Don Giovanni*, Verdi's *Ernani*, and Bellini's *Norma*, which I encourage readers to listen to and study. Nor do his more than sixty transcriptions of Schubert songs deserve anything other than the most rigorous attention. Were there enough space in these pages to lavish such attention, I would. But for now, what we can survey here will yield plenty.

Isolde's Liebestod, S. 447

Though the title of this transcription is now widely known and identified with Isolde's intoxicating final aria in act 3 of Wagner's (1813–1883) *Tristan and Isolde,* it is not an entirely accurate moniker. Wagner had originally designated it Isolde's "Verklärung" (Transfiguration). But it was in fact the opera's celebrated prelude, arguably one of the most influential compositions in the history of music, that he dubbed "Liebestod" (Love-Death).

Ironically, it was his father-in-law, Liszt, who is responsible for the generic title that survives today and that everyone knows it by in both its operatic and pianistic incarnations. Indeed, Liszt first penned his keyboard vision of Isolde's "Verklärung"—(or "Mild und leise," Soft and Gentle)—in 1867, two years after the opera's premiere, but revised and had it published anew in 1875. In those days, grand opera was accessible to the well-heeled, or to those in urban environments whose social status allowed them entry into the opera halls (which is not to say there were no exceptions); those who lived in rural areas or distant suburbs were either compelled to travel or to wait until a performance came to them.

The opening of *Liebestod* is a citation from the opera's love duet in act 2, which lingers on the words "sehnend verlangter Liebestod" (ardently longed for love-death). Four bars later, the familiar strains of Isolde's aria emerge astride a gossamer tremolando in the bass. The challenge to the pianist here is to make of its quiescent sheen something ethereal and distant; the pianist who plays it too loudly or with too much acoustic presence will ruin the moment. The tremolando, then, must shimmer rapidly in a gossamer triple *piano*, thus lending potency not to its materiality, but to its aesthetic concept.

As the cellos swell up to a D-natural, the opening segues from A-flat major to its sultry new B major theme, which is defined by a sequence of rising fourths and a chromatic descent of a half step. Here, some sixteen bars into the work, as the soprano intones over her lover Tristan's lifeless body the words "Seht ihr's nicht? Wie das Herz ihm muthig schwillt, voll und hehr im Busen ihm quillt" (Do you not see it? How his heart swells with courage, gushing and majestic in his breast?), Liszt demands that the pianist not only convey the sultry quality of the absent soprano's voice, but also the instrumentarium. The horns pulsate above a stream of triplets, gently articulated by the strings, eventually merging into a dialogue between the violins and the horns some eight bars later. A lone oboe voices its melody's circuitous ornamentation, only to be usurped, a few bars later, by the flutes and violins.

And how do pianists translate the innate qualities of these unique instruments? Well, there are any number of ways to do so, and these will depend on the manner in which pianists choreograph their physical approach to the keys, as well as pedaling, but in the final analysis it is their imagination that drives the various colors that they must at least suggest. For example, only thirty-three bars into the work, Liszt indicates asks pianists to break, or rapidly arpeggiate, the chords that inform a *pianissimo* passage. In the orchestral score, the violins are responsible for this material, which, in this transcription, moves from *pianissimo* to a triple *piano* in the uppermost register of the instrument. Savvy interpreters who combine a rigorous but seamless legato with discreetly adjudicated pedaling—pedaling, that is, that avails itself of both the sostenuto and left pedals—will create the impression of muted strings.

Thus far the entire *Liebestod* has thrived in varying degrees of *piano*, *pianissimo*, and even triple *piano*. But a volatile crescendo, which in the original invites the participation of the full orchestra, now drives the work toward its first climax in an impassioned new theme and on the words "Heller schallend, mich umwallend sind es Wellen sanfter Lüfte?" (Are they gentle aerial waves ringing out, clearly surging around me?). Absent the heaving thrusts of a dramatic soprano who would intone the text in the opera, it is now left to the pianist to convey the breathy anguish of a voice so opulent and powerful that it soars above the thickening sonorities of the orchestra.

Here the climax draws down, astride a new patch of tremolandos in broken octaves, from a ribald *fortissississimo* to a delicate *pianississimo*. A diaphanous wash of arpeggios, divided between the hands, drifts downward in imitation of a harp. The climatic theme returns but is now only a fraction of what it once was, transformed into a hollow of faded octaves in the treble. It dies away in a hush of flutes and violins, which again the pianist is entrusted to duplicate, or at least suggest, in a perpetual diminuendo and in one last tremolando in the baritone register below. At last, Isolde, exhausted, heartbroken, abandons herself to her fate, which is that of Tristan's peace, redemption, and love in the arms of death. With this, the work dies out, its chromatic ascent floating upward like the faded aroma of a decaying bouquet and dissipating astride three bars of a nearly inaudible B major arpeggio.

Given its more or less literal specificity in relation to the original, as opposed to fanciful elaboration, Liszt's *Liebestod* qualifies, at least in the view of some, as a transcription, rather than a paraphrase or a fantasy.

In the end, what really matters is the manner and success of his manipulation, shall we say, of the operatic, vocal, and symphonic music of his contemporaries and predecessors into wholly autonomous piano works. But no matter what one may call it, the *Liebestod* remains one of Liszt's most frequently played and successful compositions of the genre.

Ave Maria: A transcription from Schubert's lied

In 1838, Liszt, who had long been enamored of Schubert's music, set about to transcribe a number of that composer's most insouciant songs. By the year 1846, Liszt had transcribed nearly sixty of Schubert's songs. While preserving the essence of the originals—their harmonic profile, rhythmic organization, and formal structure—Liszt proceeded with consummate integrity in his determination to respect Schubert's aesthetic intentions. In spite of their exquisite detail, often virtuosic passagework, and colorful pianistic inventions, nowhere does he demean or disfigure the letter or the fundamental spirit of these remarkable works.

6 12 Études d'exécution transcendante, *S. 139* *(The Transcendental Études)*

If there is one musical genre that speaks to the peculiar challenges a pianist has to face, it is the étude. No one cultivated the genre to the extent that Liszt did, transforming the étude, or study, from a species of drab and mechanical reiteration to a work of musical poetry. For Liszt, the étude as genre provided innumerable opportunities: for the cultivation of myriad sonorities, for the development of piano technique in the fullest sense of that much-abused word, and for the exploration of fantasy.

But even beyond that, Liszt the showman, in the years before his retirement and in the decades before he turned his attention to more probative compositional issues, understood the new authority of the performing musician in relation to an audience. As I detailed in *Beethoven's Symphonies: A Guided Tour,* the early years of the nineteenth century saw an important new development in music that changed the relationship that, until then, had existed between the public and the performer. In the shadow of the French Revolution, music came to represent change, progress, and, above all, a means of spiritual and intellectual contemplation. Instrumental music, especially, overtook opera as an abstraction worthy of the serious-minded, who valued the symbolic, as well as the potential of art to both unite and reflect the values of a community. Music, at long last, had earned its place as an object of moral authority and intellectual weight as the public, eager to grow with the prevailing sprit of the time, engorged itself on every new significant work of art that came along. Indeed, the average music lover now welcomed music as something more than entertainment, as the monopoly that the aristocracy once had on its performance and its production diminished.

But with the death of Beethoven in 1827, and that of Schubert (whose music was relatively unknown, at least on the international stage, in his own day), things began to change. The appearance of Niccolò Paganini in Paris in 1830 inspired Liszt to re-create the piano and the pianist in the violinist's virtuoso image. That the étude could become a thing of fantasy and a correspondent to a literary ideal appealed enormously to the young composer, whose first outing in the genre was a set of conventional, even juvenile studies (Étude in Twelve Exercises, Op. 1) that he composed when he was only fifteen years old.

Liszt intuited that the pubic taste had turned and that something of music's entertainment value was again turning the heads of average audience members, if not those of the intelligentsia. Though he was not the only such concert artist to do so—Sigismond Thalberg was another celebrated virtuoso pianist and Liszt's only real rival, although his modest gifts as a composer were not so persuasive—Liszt exploited the public's new acceptance of performers as artworks in their own right, equal to the music they played. Virtuoso performers, in effect, became acolytes by virtue of the spells they could weave with music; it was a kind of hypnotism that exploited and stimulated the fascination of the masses.

Thus did audiences of the 1830s, thanks in large part to Liszt's widespread international reputation and the innovations he lent to concert presentation, become spectators whose complicity with the performer created a new kind of musical experience. Though Liszt refashioned old material to suit his developing aesthetic vision, it cannot be said that the Transcendental Études were mere rehashings of his juvenile studies, from which he appropriated certain motivic ideas, or even their earlier, similar incarnations. On the contrary, with each revision, these études, along with other works (such as the *Années de pèlerinage*), became wholly autonomous artistic entities. Each is an audacious experiment, not only in the challenges it presents for physical stamina and dexterity—things that are in essence the least of its difficulties—but in the expansion of sonorities and the evolution of musical fantasy it embraces. In these works, the performer and the work itself become one.

Though the Transcendental Études form the core of his artistic vision in the étude genre, they were hardly Liszt's only venture. Even so, it would not be an exaggeration to say that Liszt expanded the limits and potential of pianism for generations that followed. Although the Six Paganini Études, the Three Concert Études (which include the often-played "Sospiro" and the elegant "Leggierezza"), and the endearing "Waldesrauschen" (Forest Murmurs) and "Gnomenreigen" (Ride of the Gnomes) are no less important to Liszt's development, the Transcendental Études strike me as essential to any fundamental study of Liszt.

Étude No. 1 in C Major: "Preludio" (Prelude)

This bold, ebullient study serves to introduce the Transcendental Études. If it has any value for technique—though this question implies abstracting the work's physicality from its artistic merits (which is never a good idea for the substantive understanding of musical expression)—it is to warm up the pianist as much as it is to warm up the audience. It begins with a swooping arpeggio, built from a dominant seventh, that pummels from the soprano register to the bass. A chromatic surge in eights and sixteenths contradicts it and rises by stealth. A succession of chords in the left hand and broad arpeggios, in both ascent and descent, brings the work to its glamorous conclusion; the entire piece, brief and to the point, takes only a couple of minutes to complete. But again, even though the musical material may to the passive observer seem merely superficial, this is a tone poem that demands the full attention of a pianist committed to making of it a moving statement.

Étude No. 2 in *A* Minor: Molto vivace

This is one of only two études in the set that Liszt declined to give a programmatic title. Perhaps that is because its anxious, febrile character speaks for itself. It is a devilish invention, and its demeanor is that of a violin work, replete with innumerable double stops, elisions, and an overall stringlike ambience that suggests Liszt had Paganini very much on his mind when he wrote it.

Certainly, its technical demands are considerable, which is all the more reason the interpreter is obliged to come to grips with the work's no-less-considerable musical values. Cast in A minor, this étude is volatile indeed, mixing strident repeated notes with octaves and interlocking double notes. Liszt calls for all this to be engaged in a quiet dynamic—*piano*—that makes the challenges all the thornier. A wispy ascent of gossamer triplets finds no relief in the perpetual motion of alternating broken octaves and brazen chordal patterns that follow. Liszt redistributes the opening material, entrusting it first to the right and then to the left hand as the work develops. But he also exploits, with unerring vitality, the entire range of the keyboard in a punishing display of alternating double seconds, thirds, and fourths that prance from the highest to the lowest regions of the instrument. Neither the tension nor the sonorous sheen lets up for one moment, and the work concludes in a battery of octaves and rapidly rising chords.

Étude No. 3 in F Major: "Paysage" (Scenery, or Landscape)

The gentle fluidity of this bucolic confection bespeaks pastoral pleasures. Indeed, it signals as much from the outset, as does its key, F major, long a favorite tonality for composers in search of codifying landscapes. *Paysage* lulls us into its world of calm reflection, and its rhythmic symmetry in 6/8 time appeals to our senses and our aural palate. The endearing principal melody in rising octaves that inaugurates it after a four-bar introduction gives way to a fluid and wholly congenial harmonic expanse that is largely represented by four-part writing, with doublings. Its middle section enlivens the Poco adagio of the beginning, giving way to a more animated tempo and a delicate chordal progression.

There is no silence in this countryside setting, but only the overall hush of matinal imagery. Here the pianist faces many challenges, though again it is the poetic content that must be conveyed. A number of issues serve to illuminate the text, rather than cloud it. Among these are a continuous though subtle complex of articulations that demand a seasoned variety of touch, from an airy portato to a seamless legato;

an illustrative array of registrational colors, which configure distantly separated pitch material in extreme contrast; and a number of constantly changing dynamic levels that all occur within the context of *piano*. Not least, of course, is the prevailing legato, which cultivated performers will strive to accomplish, as if each of their ten fingers were an individual human voice.

"Paysage" ends much as it began—with the left hand alone giving voice to a quiescent descending melody, though now discreetly ornamented en route to its final destination, a simple F major triad.

Étude No. 4 in D Minor: "Mazeppa"

This is an impressive tone poem, which Liszt also cast in an orchestral version (as well as in an earlier pianistic incarnation, in the *Douze grandes études* of 1838). Yet another earlier version of Liszt's "Mazeppa," composed in 1840, was dedicated to Victor Hugo and appended with the title it is known by today.

A dramatic poem of Victor Hugo inspired Liszt to pen this étude. The story concerns a Ukrainian Cossack, Mazeppa, who, having been strapped to a steed, is pummeled and pounded as the horse is set free to gallop. This romantic rodeo gives way to victory, as Mazeppa earns his garland and is made a king.

Liszt's Mazeppa throws down the gauntlet with fat arpeggiated chords, which precede a breathless scalar tsunami that scampers the full length of the keyboard from bass to treble. The aggressive principal theme commences in bold triads played by both hands, but astride a sequence of ascending double thirds that fall between the strong beats. These thirds are meant to convey the clickety-clack of the horse's gallop.

However, this poses a significant physical problem for the pianist, not only due to the large leaps and the necessity to convey both continuity and rhythmic consistency in the melody, but also in consequence of the articulation. Not only are these to be played in alternation between the hands, but Liszt advised the use of a most unusual fingering in order to engender the correct articulation. Indeed, he advises the successive use of the same fingering, the index and fourth finger, on each double third, all the while alternating the hands on every other interval. Though for some pianists this would appear to make the passage more difficult, it is an ingenious solution that, when carefully adjudicated, has the opposite effect. For one thing, Liszt's fingerings compel the player to crystallize the onrush of thirds in a manner that is necessarily nonlegato, an articulation that contributes to rhythmic tension. Indeed, if there is an image conveyed here, it is that of Mazeppa at the mercy of his steed.

An artillery of interlocking octaves segues into a haunting, diaphanous middle section, wherein the melody, duly transformed, is given over to the left hand as the right gracefully surveys a parade of rising and falling double thirds. The principal theme reasserts itself in octaves as a litany of repeated double thirds and chromatic scales accompany it in the same and in the left hand. But even here, Liszt is not one to forsake musical poetry, and he writes in the score a telling instruction: "Il canto espressivo ed appassionato assai" (the melody to be played expressively and very passionately). Then, against a torrent of chromatically descending major triads, Liszt both enlivens and enriches the melodic material of the left hand en route to a restatement of the principal theme.

But once back on the radar, the theme becomes biting and sarcastic as the meter shifts from 4/4 to a devilish 6/8. In this passage, marked "allegro deciso," the horse's ever-accelerating gallop becomes visceral. Dusting the now truncated double thirds with chromatically inflected appoggiaturas, the tempo accelerates as the mood intensifies. A blaze of pounding D major triads, played by both hands, draws Mazeppa to its imperial conclusion.

Étude No. 5 in B-flat Major: "Feux follets" (Will o' the Wisps)

"Feux follets" is not only one of Liszt's more challenging études, but also one of his most endearing, at least among pianists. It difficulties are manifold, and those whose authority is substantial enough to make child's play of its litany of rapid but quiet double notes become the envy of those who cannot. The work proceeds as if to impart the pattering flutter of a butterfly in flight. Written in B-flat major, it begins with a gossamer, single-voiced, thirty-second-note brocade that ascends from the piano's middle register to a high E-flat. A no-less-transparent arpeggio astride a pattern of double thirds alights on a mischievous sixteenth-note chordal motive before the principal thematic material surges some ten bars later.

Here a chromatic array in varying double-notes—thirds, fourths, fifths, and sixths—emerges discreetly and shimmer above a simple eighth-note pattern in the tenor register below. For pianists, the physical challenges proceed not only from the swift execution of the double notes, but from imparting their character. To preserve the seamlessness of the figure, within the context of legato and *pianissimo* as Liszt commands, interpreters cannot allow the physical difficulties to compromise the musical poetry; if they do, the entire sense of the work will be lost. There can be no faking in this work. Even so, the expressive potential of each phrase holds within it the interpretive clues that can make the pianist's work somewhat easier. Liszt is careful to adjudicate the articulation, with hairpin crescendos and decrescendos, subtle accentuations, short-lived slurs, and staccato dots. What's more, where no slur is indicated—for example, there is a curious absence of long slurs over the first eight bars of the principal theme, which Liszt clearly marks legato—players would be well advised to listen to the rapidly changing harmonies in such a way as to illuminate their destiny. The figure hovers lightly, and to convey the weightlessness of so many notes, pianists must release its expressive potential and grasp its intonation. Above all, they must not play any faster than they can listen, which is to say, make note of the harmonic changes.

There is no rest in this whispering étude, and Liszt both varies and combines the principal motive with the opening salvo. A playful if somewhat diabolical deluge of lightly ornamented leaps in the left hand introduces what might be construed to be humor, which is not an entirely subjective interpretation; indeed, at this place Liszt injects "scherzando, grazioso" as a tempo, or, more adequately, as a character instruction.

Certainly, throughout this étude, the left hand, too, has its work cut out for it in more ways than one. Lightly configured octave leaps, slurred couplets in tenths, and moto perpetuum chromatic filigree and pristine arpeggios all combine to make the enchantments of the "Feux follets" something memorable and evanescent.

Étude No. 6 in G Minor: "Vision"

In stark contrast to the glittering "Feux Follets," which precedes it, "Vision" is a meditation on darker forces. There is something sinister about the opening, which so grimly pits deep double thirds against a grumbling pattern of intermittent arpeggios and an ominous, funereal pedal point in the deepest register of the bass.

The tension mounts as the harmonies enlarge to accommodate thick chords and the familiar three-note rhythmic figure so often associated with fate or death, just as in the opening of Beethoven's Fifth Symphony or the Rückblick (fourth movement) of Brahms's F Minor Piano Sonata. The expansive though brief arpeggiations alternate between the right and left hand as the work drifts from G minor to B minor, culminating in an all-consuming crescendo, as if the funeral procession, at first heard in the distance, were drawing closer.

A whoosh of arpeggios, played in unison and contrasting motion, spreads its wings over the entire range of the keyboard, only to be interrupted by the voice of doom: a dotted-note figure in repeated octaves. A cascade of *fortissimo* octaves pummels from top to bottom in anticipation of a perhaps brighter, more optimistic vision, in G major. Here a dizzying round of ascending and descending arpeggios provides a halo of sorts around the left hand, which articulates an alternating pattern of chords in the tenor and bass registers with virile intensity. The mood is nothing if not triumphant. The arpeggiations expand even more as they embrace double thirds instead of single notes above the left hand's embedded tremolando.

Gigantic chordal leaps serve to intensify the music en route to a triple *forte* cadence on a G major triad. The arpeggios return, but now embedded in a dominant seventh chord, which Liszt spells in a most unusual way (with a C-sharp rather than a D-flat). "Vision" comes to a rousing conclusion in G major with a descent of left-hand octaves and a high tremolando in the right.

Étude No. 7 in E-flat Major: "Eroica"

About all this étude bears in common with Beethoven's Third Symphony is the title. As Busoni put it, Liszt's "Eroica" is "more defiant than heroic." The florid, even bombastic introduction throws care to the winds, emerging from a violent array of diminished chords that leap from the middle to the lower to the upper register of the piano in the first bar alone. A scintillating, southward-sweeping arpeggio lays down the law in the second measure, only to be reprimanded by another, rising chordal figure.

The principal theme, a confident march in the work's home key of E-flat major, belted out by the left hand in strident octaves, commences some twenty bars into the work. Indeed, as "Eroica" proceeds, octaves rule the day, until Liszt refashions it as a single line in the middle register, harmonized by broken chords below it. Later still, the intricate arpeggiations of the opening combine with the principal theme, which is now entrusted to the left hand in octaves, while an eighth-note accompaniment, in the same hand, ambles quietly in the lower end of the bass. Pianists, then, must exercise a certain stoic calm throughout this work if they are to succeed in conveying its expressive power. Pianists who mistake leaping for jumping will be in trouble, as the former is an approach to the physicality of the passage that will result only in wrong notes. Leaping, on the other hand, is best executed in the context of a glide, with the hand remaining close to the keys as if in the graceful motion of a glissando.

An impressive array of parallel octaves then yield their *fortissimo* burden with precisely the bravura Liszt advises in the score. The result is what in German is called *Schwung*, or swing; like an immense, leaden pendulum, these octaves sway back and forth, up and down as they outline the prevailing harmonic goal points, which in this case are chords on B-flat major, E-flat minor, F minor, A-flat major, and A-flat minor. The coda revisits both the octave pattern of the principal theme and the chordal leaps and descending arpeggios of the introduction. The work ends, as expected, in a confident expression of *fortissimo* octaves and the imposition of thickly configured dominant and tonic chords.

Étude No. 8 in C Minor: "Wilde Jagd" (Wild Hunt)

If ever there was a case to make for the recurrence of Sturm und Drang as a concept, at least in music of the romantic era, "Wilde Jagd" certainly provides it. The tempo marking of "presto furioso" contributes to the sheer physicality of this work, which requires pianists to manage their energy with care; no matter its relatively brief length, "Wilde Jagd" is a tour de force that demands considerable stamina from players who hope to master it.

Liszt has simplified this, his last version of "Wilde Jagd." In its earlier incarnation of 1837, he cast it in a fundamental sonata form. But here, what had been a recapitulation in the earlier version has been removed and replaced by a rousing coda of thickening chords and blustery double-note arpeggios.

The work begins in C minor with a pattern of alternating octaves and single notes in the bass, which leap into an array of dotted notes. These Liszt configures as a procession of thick chords played in unison by both hands. Set in 6/8 time, the entire work sports something of the character of a tarantella. A splay of chromatic scales thrusts itself downward with lightning speed into the overwhelming, and entirely unexpected silence of a whole-bar rest lengthened by a fermata.

A vigorous, sputtering chordal figure, framed and intermittently interrupted by a contrasting pattern of rocket-fire thirty-second-notes, emerges soon enough. But then a playful dotted figure in thirds introduces the horn calls of the hunt. Here the key has migrated to E-flat major, conveying the cheerful bustle and ambience that horns, were this an orchestral transcription, would surely suggest. The mood grows more playful still as wide chordal leaps inform the dotted rhythm that sustains the étude's bountiful energy.

Now we hear a lyrical if nervous second subject, related to the first (thus essentially showing this work to be a monothematic invention). Its four-bar phrases are punctuated by a pointed dotted figure in the left hand that morphs into treacherous two-octave leaps as the right hand takes off above it. A powerful triple-*forte* climax brings the thematic content of the second subject into the upper reaches of the keyboard as the left hand issues chordal syncopes below. Things turn brighter still in the C major section that follows, wherein the dotted figure, now cast as a pattern of sixteenth-note C major triads in 2/4 time, alternates in dialogue between the hands.

A parade of widely spaced octave leaps in the right hand imparts something of a sarcastic patina to the proceedings as the left hand goes about its business in dotted double thirds. The lyrical second subject makes one last appearance; its tempo remains agitated, but now it purrs in *piano*. Liszt again imposes triple *forte* for the coda, which rejects the previous metrical division in six for a more svelte 2/4 time. The final bars assume a downward plunge of staccatissimo chords in the right hand and a rotation of octaves in the left. The hunt over, "Wilde Jagd" concludes with an abbreviated sixteenth-note recall of the étude's opening figure, now played in unison in the bass and lunging with determination onto the final C minor triad.

Étude No. 9 in A-flat Major: "Ricordanza" (Remembrance)

The elaborate Italianate confection that is "Ricordanza" brings Liszt back to the Italy of *Années de pèlerinage*. The bel canto profusion that inaugurates the work will already be familiar to those who know Liszt's Petrarch Sonnets, which likewise take their inspiration from operatic models. Here Liszt spins out an opulent, long-limbed, and highly ornamented theme (though the ornaments are all written out) in the tenor register. It is no accident that he indicates the tempo as andantino, but not without modifying it parenthetically with improvisato (like an improvisation).

A series of cadenzas, lengthy florid roulades, and lightly detached arpeggios weaves a world of enchantments. The fundament of the principal melody is simple enough: a dotted quarter-note followed by three eighths, a pattern Liszt will repeat throughout. Indeed, only twenty bars into the work, he transforms it into a halting, deftly syncopated variant that is accompanied, in the left hand, by double notes. The theme then expands into another variant in octaves, before moving on to a delicate procession of double notes in the soprano register. A gentle cascade of arpeggios, played by the left hand, enriches the melody, now tossed ever so gently to the right. A wash of ascending and descending right-hand arpeggios engages the theme, which is now given prominent if quiet voice in the left.

Liszt resumes the syncopated elaboration of the theme before recasting it with a certain gravitas in the alto register astride a pulsation of dense repeated chords in the bass. The étude continues its journey with a whirlwind of arpeggio brocades before expanding the theme into a boldly stated variant in *fortissimo* octaves. The theme returns in the bass, quietly surrounded by evanescent arpeggios, which envelop it like a halo. Finally, "Ricordanza" drifts off into a brief remnant of its principal theme and fades away on three arpeggiated tonic chords.

Étude No. 10 in F Minor: Allegro agitato molto (CD Track 5)

Though it has no programmatic title, this intriguing Étude in F minor invites any number of colorful interpretations. Busoni suggested that it ought to be called appassionato and to leave it at that. The piece starts in a tangled descent of interlocking triads. These alight only a bar and a half later on the principal theme, which pulsates breathlessly in a succession of chromatic, slurred duplets. In imitation of a sigh, these are configured in the context and on the margins of triplets, which alternate between the hands. Only five bars into the work, the intervallic dimensions expand as the octaves move upward by a minor sixth.

Combining the octave theme, its urgency increasing every moment, with a stream of widely distended triplets in the bass left hand below, Liszt builds both harmonic and rhythmic tension with cumulative intensity. A second theme in C-flat major offers a clarion call of sorts; it commences in the upper register of the piano with a salvo of repeated octaves that saunter upward, first to G-flat and then to G-sharp, in stepwise motion. A return of the interlocking chords precedes a new variant of the second theme, which is now thrown to the left hand as a vigorous arpeggiation rides alongside it in the right.

Then a string of parallel chords moves chromatically upward, and in contrary motion to a succession of arpeggiated chords below, culminating in a brilliant *fortissimo* climax that dissolves into a rapidly descending D-flat major arpeggio. As the arpeggios fall to the bass, Liszt exploits the work's 6/8 meter in a manner similar to the concluding section of the Mephisto Waltz No. 1, written some ten years later. The music waxes diabolical as it hobbles goat footed; making matters even more complicated for the performer, the hands alternate with staccato duplets that are out of sync with each other. Marked "tempestoso," they form a stormy episode indeed.

The alternating material of the opening returns, as does the principal sighing theme. But things grow even more restless en route to a searing climax that zeroes in on a string of repeated octaves on D-flat, which then drop off into falling syncopes before resuming, yet gain, the sighing motive. For the pianist, the left hand here is punishing and can be exhausting if played mechanically. The large and frequent leaps that articulate its trajectory notwithstanding, it remains a harmonically rich accompaniment that must project a no-less-melodic attitude than the theme it surrounds. Thus, even in a figure as evidently tumultuous and difficult at this, affective inflection of its harmonic contrasts—particularly the constituents that contribute to dissonance—is indispensable.

Following a repetition of the opening thematic figurations, and a compelling sequence of wide arpeggiated chords in contrary motion, the coda engages in diminution of the principal theme—that is, its restatement in shorter note values—that moves headlong in a relentless frenzy toward a blustery conclusion of leaping octaves and brazen dominant and tonic chords.

Étude No. 11 in D-flat Major: "Harmonies du soir" (Evening Harmonies)

This alluring work, a tone poème disguised as an étude, is the culmination of Liszt's original vision expressed in his earliest set of studies, the Étude in Twelve Exercises, Op. 1. But here the pretensions of the child Liszt have been banished in favor of the mature probity of a master composer.

"Harmonies du soir" proffers mystery as its aesthetic capital. But this is the mystery of colorful sonorities that hemorrhage one into another as they come into gradual focus. The work begins impressionistically enough, in an ambiguous harmonic haze atop a dominant pedal point in the home key of D-flat major. The wanderlust of the opening chordal procession in eighth-notes is rendered all the more intriguing by the cadential character for the irresolute derived dominants that inform it. The opulent principal theme, assumed by the left hand in a profusion of efflorescent chords in the baritone and tenor registers, opens up as if onto a spacious vista. Widely spaced broken chords, assimilating themselves as distinct arpeggiations, emerge in the right hand as they proffer the thematic design anew. These in turn broaden into a passionate expanse of broken chords in advance of a change of key, to E major.

A new melodic idea, issued within the dynamic context of a whispering *pianississimo*, takes shape in G major. Though its rhythmic and even textural design is a procession of chords that stream along in eighth-notes, its mood is perhaps less discreet. As it expands above a roll of G major and then D major arpeggiations below, it draws the listener into its orbit, as if it were falling irresistibly into a particularly magnetic gravitational field. As the tonality migrates to C major and then to an even brighter key, B major, the dynamic intensifies to a majestic *fortissimo*. A swift decrescendo returns the music to triple *piano* and an eerie ascent on the dominant pitch, B, which is repeated across four octaves.

An operatic second subject in E major emerges out of a brief interim of silence. It is a memorable and impassioned canto broadcast in the alto register. This impassioned pianistic arioso sets two eight-bar phrases side by side, its declamation made all the more inflamed by the thrilling leaps of broken octaves that divide over the bar lines, from upbeat to downbeat.

With this, a triumphant restatement of the broad second subject ingratiates in a pastiche of gigantic chords, played *fortissimo*. In support, the left hand, too, grabs hold of a repeated chordal configuration and then, two bars later, of broken octaves, which scamper in large leaps up and down the keyboard in triplets. Interlocking octaves lead to a return to D-flat major, where the lyrical bel canto that was the third subject is now transformed into a gargantuan profusion of octave doublings in the soprano and bass registers. These in turn are enriched by thick, multivoiced chordal configurations in the middle registers. As the middle voices intensify the mood with a relentless chromatic ascent, the effect is startling, bringing to mind not merely the three-handed effect for which Liszt became famous in his youth, but something even greater. To be sure, to achieve the rich sonorities that the music demands, the pianist is obliged to differentiate the dynamic levels so as not to blandly equalize the passage's multiple constituents.

Just as one thinks things cannot possibly get any louder, they do. But volume is not the key in this étude: largesse and richness of tone are. If there is one glaring obstacle to an effective performance of "Harmonies du soir," it is precisely that: the interpretation of relative dynamics and contrasts. Pounding the keys with merciless abandon will do nothing to enrich the sound but, on the contrary, will serve only to obliterate a subtle array of slightly differentiated colorations within the chords, as well as attenuate drama and intensity.

The étude winds down, after a sudden diminuendo, and spreads itself over three bars on the wings of sotto voce dominant and tonic chords and what has by now become the expected complement of left-hand arpeggiations. Mystery returns to the proceedings as a fluid ascent, a variant of the first subject, soars and alights again on a sequence of widely spaced broken chords. As these enlarge to an arpeggiated D-flat major chord, the work droops, tranquil and accepting, to its modest conclusion.

Étude No. 12 in B-flat Minor: "Chasse-neige" (The Snow Squall)

"Chasse-neige" paints a wintry landscape in the chilly tremolandos and the gentle descent of its principal theme. The title has an interesting background, especially in light of what it later came to mean in everyday French: a snow plow. Indeed, that's precisely what the work often sounds like in the heavy hands of mediocre or simply incompetent pianists. It was not until 1878 that the modern-day meaning was coined in association with a new invention, attached to the front of a horse-drawn carriage or a train, used for clearing snow. But in 1834 its meaning was something else entirely, as it referred to a snowstorm or the blustery wind that accompanies such a deluge. Alexandre Dumas's 1859 poem "Le chasse-neige" is a case in point, as it is more often than not translated simply as "Snow Squall."

Large octave leaps, which span several octaves, grow out of the tremolandos and mingle effortlessly with the vibratory accompaniment.

Liszt creates a mood at once compelling and austere. The key is B-flat minor, a bright tonality that seems particularly well suited to the atmosphere Liszt hopes to convey.

The tremolos, which inexorably morph into more complex and interlocking chordal patterns, present substantial, if not insurmountable, physical difficulties. To maintain the essential quiescence of their fluttering presence without compromising the affective expressiveness of the melodic figuration is no easy task and demands a listening apparatus in tune with the a work's programmatic narrative and fragile pianistic topography.

A patch of rising and falling chromatic scales, played by the left hand in swift succession, brings cooler winds to the musical patina, but even the scales expand exponentially into a decorative free fall evocative of a biting gust. What follows is a treacherous episode configured as enormous leaps of octaves and sixths in both hands that again segues into a lengthy ascending chromatic ascent, which, at its apex, parts the compositional waters as it sets out in contrary motion.

In the work's final measures, Liszt combines the chromatic figurations with the principal theme, now cast in pairs of slurred double thirds. An onrush of B-flat minor chords in alternation mounts upward to the highest register of the piano, only to drop definitively onto a sforzando tonic triad. And with that, this and all the Transcendental Études come to their precipitous close.

Glossary

accelerando — A gradual heightening, or cumulative quickening, of tempo.

adagio — A slow tempo, but neither turgid nor comatose. An adagio must move, broadly.

affect — Comes from the *Affektenlehre,* or Doctrine of Affects, a seventeenth-century aesthetic ideology that the emotions could be codified in sound and that a rhetorical grammar of such affections could be made part of compositional procedure. Though the terms are not exactly interchangeable, it is a species of *inflection* and is best described as referring to the degree of emphasis, dynamic weight, or perspective performers invest in any given motivic figuration.

allegretto — A lively, quick, and above all playful tempo, but not quite so fast as allegro.

allegro — Generally understood to be a fast or moderately fast tempo, but in music of the baroque and classical eras, especially, it refers to character and disposition; it can be construed to mean "cheerful" or "happy."

andante — A gracious walking tempo, not too slow nor too quick. Subject to any number of gradations.

articulation — The manner in which a performer distinguishes, by means of attack, prolongation, and release, certain tones, motives, phrases, and groups of pitches individually and in relation to one another. Composers either spell out or provide symbols to indicate types of articulation—for example, staccato, legato, wedges, tenuto, and other accent marks.

baroque music Music composed roughly between 1590 and 1750 that embraces certain styles and techniques attributable to the aesthetic ideas, formulations, and philosophy of the time. Due to its long run, the baroque era is usually divided into three distinct periods of its own, each governed by specific innovations. Opera, the fugue, and the harmonization of a ground bass were products of baroque invention.

cadence That which harmonically demarcates and provides a sense of resolution, with varying degrees of finality, at the end of a phrase or larger section of a work. In its harmonic tendency to move back toward the key of the work, cadence is also an expression of a composition's tonality.

cadenza Usually, but not only, found in a concerto. An extended solo passage toward the end of a concerto or sonata form, before the coda, that elaborates and ornaments the principal themes of the work with a view toward showing off the skill of its composer, or soloist, or both. Although composers sometimes write out the cadenza, performers, too, occasionally write their own.

canon A musical pattern defined by a thematic subject that is presented, then successively imitated by one or more voices commencing on different pitches. There are different kinds of canon: fixed, which is imitation by rote; and free, which introduces modifications of pitch material and rhythm.

classical era The period of musical composition that extended from the early eighteenth century through the early nineteenth century. Its exact division into years is difficult to measure, as classicism evolved slowly and its attendant techniques and aesthetics eventually bled into romanticism. Characteristic of music of the classical era is periodic phrasing, longer harmonic rhythms, simpler, more natural melodic designs, homophonic textures, greater use of specifically marked dynamic contrasts, et cetera.

coda — The concluding section of a movement or single composition, which usually encapsulates the work's principal themes. A coda may be as brief as a few measures, or elaborate and extensive.

counterpoint — The simultaneous unfolding of two or more melodies, and the various compositional principles that govern their existence and formulation—that is, their movement apart or away from each other, their rhythmic differences, and the resultant harmonies they create in relation to each other.

crescendo, decrescendo — A gradual, cumulative increase or decrease in volume indicated by hairpins signs or written out by the composer. This intensification of sound in either direction informs the affective character of the passage it modifies.

cyclic form — A technique of musical construction, involving multiple sections or movements, in which a theme, melody, or thematic material occurs in more than one movement as a unifying device.

czardas — A traditional Hungarian dance, accompanied by Gypsy music in 2/4 or 4/4 time with compelling syncopated rhythms.

development — The middle section of a movement in sonata form, wherein the principal themes and motivic ideas are varied, elaborated, intensified, and ornamented, en route to the recapitulation.

dominant — Every major and minor scale consists of seven pitches; the fifth degree of the scale is called the dominant. A chord constructed around this pitch includes the seventh degree of the scale. The tendency of the seventh degree to move toward its neighboring tonic pitch is strong and creates a feeling of expectation and desire for resolution in its listeners.

diminution — The presentation of a melody in note values shorter than those in which it was originally cast.

dominant — Refers to pitch, chord, or tonality that is based on the fifth degree of a major or minor scale; often resolves onto the tonic. When based on the dominant of a scale degree other than the tonic, it is called a *secondary dominant*.

dotted notes — A dot placed just alongside a pitch increases the temporal value of that note by one-half of its original value. Two dots set in this way increase the value by yet another quarter of that value.

exposition — The first section of a sonata, in which the principal themes of the compositions are presented in juxtaposition one to the other, and including at least one major modulation to a secondary key, most often but not necessarily the dominant.

friss — The fast section of the czardas, a Hungarian folk dance. The term is used to describe most of Liszt's Hungarian Rhapsodies, which take their form from this dance. The friss can be turbulent or jubilant in tone.

fugue — A composition in which a theme (also known as a subject) is stated and then repeated consecutively in two or more voices in imitative counterpoint. This confluence of voices is then elaborated, extended, varied, modulated, developed in any number of ways.

fugato	A usually brief contrapuntal section that occurs within a sonata movement or other form and that, while at once contrapuntal and imitative—the essential elements of a fugue—does not develop into a full-blown fugue.
intonatsiia	A Russian concept that defines intervallic relationships both in theory and in performance, assigning implicit tension to the space that divides one pitch from another (when distended successively) as a matter of determinate perspective.
lento	Slow.
mediant	Refers to a pitch, chord, or tonality based on the third degree of a major or minor scale.
motive, motif	A brief rhythmic systole of a specific duration and design that attains to its own identity and becomes the basis of more elaborate structures, movements, and whole works.
Neapolitan sixth	A chromatically inflected inverted triad (that is, where the third of the chord, instead of assuming its place in the middle of the triad, becomes the lowest-sounding pitch), in major or minor, which is based on the lowered second degree of the scale. E.g., in C major, the Neapolitan sixth is based on D-flat, with F-natural as the lowest pitch.
ostinato	A repetitive rhythmic and melodic pattern reiterated over the course of a composition, usually carried in the bass.
pedal point	A single tone, reiterated and sustained under changing harmonic patterns and over an extended period. While pedal points frequently occur in the bass, they can also be dispatched in any voice to enhance harmonic and rhythmic tension.
piano; pianissimo	Soft; very soft.

più animato	More animated, livelier.
pizzicato	In string instruments, an articulation wherein the string is plucked with the fingers rather than bowed.
polyphony	Wherein several musical voices, or lines, are heard in combination, and where each line has an independent character.
presto; *prestissimo*	Very fast; faster still than presto.
recapitulation	In sonata form, the concluding section of a movement, wherein all the principal themes of the work are restated, usually in the tonic key.
sforzando	A sudden, interruptive accentuation.
sonata form	The traditional form used most often in a work's first movement, but also in other movements in instrumental music of the classical period and beyond. Though it can be identified by a few standard organizational procedures—exposition, development, and recapitulation, as well as key relationships that juxtapose tonic and dominant in the first section, et cetera—it is best viewed as a dynamic process.
staccato	The distinct separation of the pitch it modifies from its neighboring notes. From the baroque era onward, staccato was an articulation marking, indicated by a dot above the note that instructed the player to cancel the prevailing legato.
stringendo	A tempo instruction indicating that the passage it modifies should become progressively faster.
subdominant	Refers to a pitch, chord, or tonality based on the fourth degree of a major or minor scale.
submediant	Refers to a pitch, chord, or tonality based on the sixth degree of a major or minor scale.

syncope (short for syncopation)
: A temporary shift of accentuation that contradicts the metrical organization within a bar line or phrase, though the metrical identity of the passage stays intact. For example, an accent on a weak beat of a bar on the heels of unaccented strong beat will modify the function of those beats, turning a weak beat into a strong beat, and can thus affect harmonic orientation, articulation, and rhythmic trajectory.

tempo
: The rate of speed at which a piece of music is played; a specific tempo is indicated by the composer, who relies on a performer to respect tempo instructions according to the universally understood precepts and in accordance with contemporary performance practice.

thematic transformation
: A compositional process whereby a theme is altered, manipulated, and varied in such a way as to maintain its identity yet change its character.

tonality
: The organization of tones around a single central pitch, or *tonic*. Tonality comprises all twelve major and minor keys, as well as the scales, triads, and harmonic functions that define them.

tremolo
: The rapid repetition or rapid alternation of a single pitch, group of pitches, or chord. Used for purposes of affective and dramatic intensification.

triplet
: Three notes of equal value played in place of two notes of equal value.

CD Track Listing

1. Sonata in B Minor (29:33)
   (C.W. Post College, L.I., New York, Jan. 3, 1976)

2. "Dante" Sonata (18:13)
   (92nd Street YMHA, New York, Feb. 24, 1981)

3. *Jeux d'Eau a la Ville d'Este* (9:02)
   (Masonic Auditorium, San Francisco, Feb. 25, 1979)

4. Ballade No. 2 (14:27)
   (Masonic Auditorium, San Francisco, Feb. 25, 1979)

5. Transcendental Etude No. 10 (4:52)
   (Philharmonic Hall, New York, Feb. 15, 1970)

Claudio Arrau Plays Liszt
Public Performances [1970–1981]
From Music & Arts CD-1205

Thanks to Chris Arrau and the Estate of Claudio Arrau
for authorizing this release.

UNLOCKING THE MASTERS

The highly acclaimed Unlocking the Masters series brings rec into the world of the greatest composers and their music. All b come with CDs that have tracks taken from the world's fore libraries of recorded classics, bringing the music to life.

"With infectious enthusiasm and keen insight, the Unlocking Masters series succeeds in opening our eyes, ears, hearts, and m to the great composers." – *Strings*

BEETHOVEN'S SYMPHONIES: A LISTENER'S GUIDE
by John Bell Young
US $22.95 • 978-1-57467-169-8 • HL00331951

BRAHMS: A LISTENER'S GUIDE
by John Bell Young
US $22.95 • 978-1-57467-171-1• HL00331974

CHOPIN: A LISTENER'S GUIDE TO THE MASTER OF THE PIANO
by Victor Lederer
US $22.95 • 978-1-57467-148-3 • HL00331699

DEBUSSY: THE QUIET REVOLUTIONARY
by Victor Lederer
US $22.95 • 978-1-57467-153-7 • HL00331743

DVOŘÁK: ROMANTIC MUSIC'S MOST VERSATILE GENIUS
by David Hurwitz
US $27.95 • 978-1-57467-107-0 • HL00331662

THE GREAT INSTRUMENTAL WORKS
by M. Owen Lee
US $27.95 • 978-1-57467-117-9 • HL00331672

EXPLORING HAYDN: A LISTENER'S GUIDE TO MUSIC'S BOLDEST INNOVATOR
by David Hurwitz
US $27.95 • 978-1-57467-116-2 • HL00331671

LISZT: A LISTENER'S GUIDE
by John Bell Young
US $22.99 • 978-1-57467-170-4 • HL00331952

THE MAHLER SYMPHONIES: AN OWNER'S MANUAL
by David Hurwitz
US $22.95 • 978-1-57467-099-8 • HL00331650

OPERA'S FIRST MASTER: THE MUSICAL DRAMAS OF CLAUDIO MONTEVERDI
by Mark Ringer
US $29.95 • 978-1-57467-110-0 • HL00331665

GETTING THE MOST OUT OF MOZART: THE VOCAL WORKS
by David Hurwitz
US $22.95 • 978-1-57467-106-3 • HL0033166

GETTING THE MOST OUT OF MOZART: THE INSTRUMENTAL WORKS
by David Hurwitz
US $22.95 • 978-1-57467-096-7 • HL0033164

PUCCINI: A LISTENER'S GUIDE
by John Bell Young
US $22.95 • 978-1-57467-172-8 • HL0033197

SHOSTAKOVICH SYMPHONIES AND CONCERTO AN OWNER'S MANUAL
by David Hurwitz
US $22.95 • 978-1-57467-131-5 • HL0033169

SIBELIUS, THE ORCHESTRAL WORKS: AN OWNER'S MANUAL
by David Hurwitz
US $27.95 • 978-1-57467-149-0 • HL0033173

TCHAIKOVSKY: A LISTENER'S GUIDE
by Daniel Felsenfeld
US $27.95 • 978-1-57467-134-6 • HL0033169

DECODING WAGNER: AN INVITATION TO HIS WORLD OF MUSIC DRAMA
by Thomas May
US $27.95 • 978-1-57467-097-4 • HL0033164

www.amadeuspress.com
Prices and availability subject to change without notice.